Keys To Becoming a Victorious Woman

Lessons Learned

from

Women of the Bible

BRENDA K. FIELDS

May you find your
place of victory in that

Brenda Fields

Keys To Becoming a Victorious Woman

Copyright © 2015 by Brenda K. Fields

ISBN 978-1-942814-00-9

Cover Design: Donna Osborn Clark at www.CreationByDonna.com

Layout and Interior Design: CreationsByDonna@gmail.com

Editing: Shell Vera at www.eyesstraightahead.com

Published by: Kingdom Connection Publications

For information on booking or to contact the Author:
Email: AuthorBrendaFields@gmail.com
Facebook: Author Brenda Fields
Fax: 1-866-823-5529

Dedication

This book is dedicated to my parents, the late Elder Eugene Fields and Mrs. Beulah Fields, for introducing me to Christ and demonstrating godliness in their lifestyles.

Thank You

To Apostle LaMar and Sheila McKnight for your support and encouragement.

To my family and friends who believed in and encouraged me along the way.

Preface

As I journey through life, I continuously have a quest to be victorious in every stage. My desire has always been to please God and have delight in His sight. Psalms 37:4 says if we delight ourselves in the Lord He will give us the desires of our heart. As I gained a better understanding of God's Word, I began to gain more of an understanding of His desire to see us, His daughters, be victorious in every endeavor we pursue. A victory for us is a victory for God; He's rooting for us; cheering us on and encouraging us to move forwards towards victory every step of the way.

God wants us to be victorious throughout every phase of our lives. To accomplish this we must focus on delighting our Heavenly Father and adapting His Godly character into our lifestyle. As I seek to identify the keys to victorious living, I am constantly drawn to the many examples set by women within the Bible. There are many women throughout the Bible who were victorious and demonstrated characteristics that if we would adapt in our lives, would guide us on to victory and delight in the sight of God. In this study of victorious women within the Bible, I will focus on numerous women who left their marks in Biblical history by exemplifying character that led them, and can lead us, to victory.

My prayer for each of you reading these words is that you will adapt these characteristics in your life and become the woman God created you to be by fulfilling your calling and obtaining victory in every area.

Introduction

Working as a Manager has taught me the importance of having our Heavenly Father on my side. We as women, whether working in corporate America or within our households, face many decisions and responsibilities throughout our day that would be overwhelming without God. The realization that God is with me and He wants me to be victorious in every area of my life is the thing that gives me the courage to move forward toward my destiny. He wants me to prosper in everything to which I put my hands. He wants me to be the head and not the tail, a leader and not always a follower.

God has given us the keys to victory through the many examples demonstrated by women in the Bible. If we follow the example these women provided us, we too will be victorious. I have always sought books and workshops to help me grow and be successful in my role as a Manager within corporate America. We have many great teachers of leadership principles but I have found that the principles taught by God outweigh them all. God has presented women in the Bible to teach us life lessons that are applicable to and still bring victory to the doers today. This study will introduce to some and reiterates to others proven, fail-proof keys to acquire success in every area of life. This book is for women who desire guidance on proven principles to become successful in their careers, marriages, families, ministries and all other relationships in their lives. So daughters of God, I encourage you to sit back, make yourself comfortable and enjoy reading these proven keys that will help you climb the ladder of success and become a victorious woman in God.

Table of Contents

Workbook & Daily Journal

Keys to Becoming a Victorious Woman

Lessons Learned from Women of the Bible

Total Submission
to God's Plan for Your Life

I have been crucified with Christ; it is no longer I who live, but Christ lives in me; and the life which I now live in the flesh I live by faith in the Son of God, who loved me and gave Himself for me. Galatians 2:20

This first woman I would like to discuss teaches us our most important lesson. She was the chosen vessel by God to become the Mother of our Savior Jesus Christ: Mary. The Bible doesn't speak much of Mary's life before being chosen to bear the Savior of the world, but we can imagine the character she must have exhibited and the love she must have had for God to have such great honor bestowed upon her. Luke describes Mary's initial message from and response to the Angel Gabriel upon being informed of God's plan for her life. In Luke 1:28, the Angel Gabriel's greeted Mary with, "Rejoice, highly favored one, the Lord is with you; blessed are you among women!" What a salutation to be labeled highly favored of God, having God "be with you" and being blessed among all other women. Gabriel proceeded to tell Mary that she has been chosen to bear the Son of God, Jesus Christ, as a virgin. Mary questioned him, wondering how His prophecy could be true considering virgins cannot conceive. Gabriel then, in Luke 1:35, explained to her, "The Holy Spirit will come upon you, and the power of the Highest will overshadow you; therefore, also, that Holy One who is to be born will be called the Son of God." Mary responds, "Behold the maidservant of the Lord! Let it be to me according to your word."

Mary's response reflects one of the most important character traits that we as women must have to be victorious in our life and gain the favor of God: total submission of our lives to God's plan. Now, I know that some of you may be wondering, "Who wouldn't want to bear the Savior of the world?" You were not called to bear the Savior of the world, but there have been many times you were called by God to do something. What was your response to him? Whether that calling was teaching His Word, winning lost souls, singing in the choir or ushering at the doors your response and dedication to your God given responsibility reflects your level of submission to God. If we can't fully dedicate ourselves to what God has assigned us to do, whether a temporary calling or a lifelong responsibility, how can we even compare ourselves to Mary who surrendered her all to God?

Mary was engaged to Joseph, a carpenter—a great catch for any single women. To all of the single women reading this, imagine the excitement Mary was feeling being engaged to a Man of God—a gentleman who respects her as a Woman of God. How do we know that Joseph respected Mary? She was still a virgin but when he found out that she was pregnant,

Matthew 1:19 says that, "Joseph her husband, being a just man, and not wanting to make her a public example, was minded to put her away secretly." Even after finding out that she was pregnant he loved her enough to not expose what at that time would be perceived as a sin.

How many single women, after waiting for "the one" after all these years, would be willing to give up on marriage to bear a child for God? How many would be willing to forsake "the one" to go and work on the mission fields in another country or to totally submit to God's calling on her life. Mary was willing to give it all up to surrender to God and fulfill His calling on her life. As women of God we must submit as maidservants before our Heavenly Father, putting His plan and desires for us as our number one priority. Mary was not concerned with losing Joseph or with the criticism she would have to face being an unwed Mother. Can you imagine having to explain to a judgmental world that you did not sin but are instead bearing the child of God, the Savior of the world? Who would have believed you?

Women in those times were stoned to death for adultery but Mary was only concerned with fulfilling God's plan for her as the maidservant of her Lord. I am sure that Mary had started planning the wedding, imagined becoming a wife, a mother and living happily ever after in a nice beautiful home built by her future husband Joseph, the carpenter. Then God came along and interrupted her plans with His plan.

Can you remember a time in your life when you had things all planned out only to find that God had other plans for you? What was your response? Your response to God's interruptions in your life reflects your level of submission to Him and your trust of His plan for your life. Our willingness to lay aside our plans for God's plan requires our total trust in God and a spiritual revelation that God always has our best interest in mind. We as daughters of God must be willing to lay aside our plans for God's plan so we can live the best life that Father God has to offer us.

To be a victorious woman of God our first desire must be to fulfill God's divine purpose for our life. God's plan for us must come before our desire for a husband, a wedding, children, mansions, money, career, friends, family and anything else you can think of. There is always victory at the end for those who totally submit to the will of God. God came that we might have an abundant life and that we might abound in all things. You will never lose when you put God first. As we see in Mary's life, she did not lose Joseph as her husband nor did she miss out on having other children, she gained more than she could have ever imagined. In Luke 1:46-55 we read the song of Mary; an expression of her joy in being chosen by God to bear Christ.

And Mary said, "My soul magnifies the Lord, and my spirit has rejoiced in God my Savior. For He has regarded the lowly state of His maidservant; for behold, henceforth all generations will call me blessed. For He who is mighty has done great things for me, and holy is His name. And His mercy is on those who fear Him from generation to generation. He has shown strength with His arm; He has scattered the proud in the imagination of their hearts. He has put down the mighty from their thrones, and exalted the lowly. He has filled the hungry with good things, and the rich He has sent away empty. He has helped His servant Israel, in remembrance of His mercy, as He spoke to our fathers, to Abraham and to his seed forever."

Note in Luke 1:48 Mary sings that all generations shall call her blessed, for He that is mighty has done great things for me. Thousands of years have passed and to this day we continue to call Mary blessed. When you totally surrender your will to God's will women throughout future generations will look back at your life, call you blessed and know that the favor of God was upon you.

Daughters of God, let me encourage you to examine your life and identify those areas in which you have not totally surrendered to God. Upon honest examination I guarantee that you will agree you have not received God's best in those areas whether in your marriage, career, family or ministry. God desires our total surrender to Him in every area of our life. I am sure that Mary never imagined the honor that was bestowed upon her. She knew that the Savior was coming but I am sure she never imagined He was coming through her. People thought that the Savior would come through other means but God chose the Virgin Mary to bear the Savior.

Regardless of your status in life or your prior history, when you totally surrender to God, He will take you further than you could ever imagine. How would your marriage look if you totally surrendered it to God? Where would your career or business be if you totally surrendered to God? What type employee would your boss see you as if you totally surrendered to be the employee who delights in God and His will? My challenge to you today is that you totally submit your life to God. When you totally submit to God your victory is guaranteed. This requires that you allow God's will to take priority in every area of your life. For eyes have not seen nor ears heard the great heights that you will go and the great exploits that God will accomplish through you when you totally surrender to His will (1 Corinthians 2:9).

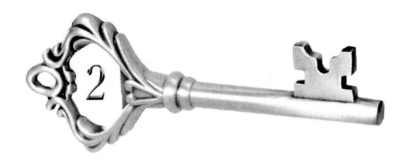

Daily Communion with God

Behold, I stand at the door and knock. If anyone hears My voice and opens the door, I will come in to him and dine with him, and he with Me. Revelation 3:20

I asked a dear friend of mine who has owned a successful business for more than 25 years what is the one thing that Christian women need to do to be victorious in their lives. Her response was to put God first everyday regardless of how busy you are. Many times we as women become so consumed with our responsibilities that we neglect spending personal time with God our Savior. Our Heavenly Father yearns for us to commune with Him seeking directions and instructions for our daily walk. Our having communion with Him is so important that He sent His only begotten son to the earth to die as a sacrifice to restore the relationship that was lost through Adams sin.

So many of us have allowed this benefit of communion with God to become so common that we no longer appreciate it or the price that was paid for us to have the right go before our Heavenly Father. We become so consumed in our daily routine, which oftentimes doesn't include spending quality time with God. We get up, get dressed, get the kids ready for school, get breakfast on the table and ensure everyone arrives at their destinations on time. If we as women would only take time to remember that it is God who has blessed us with our families, our jobs, the ability to dress ourselves and get to our destinations safely and unharmed then maybe we would fit the time in our day to just say, "Thank you God." If we would remember that our God is all powerful and all knowing, maybe we would fit time into our busy schedules to go before Him daily before we do anything else to seek His guidance and direction for our day.

The Prophetess Anna in Luke 2:36-39 demonstrated this key to victorious living: Anna served God daily with fasting and prayers. Her fasting and daily communions with God made her sensitive to the recognition of Christ the Savior when His parents bought Him into the temple. As we commune with God daily we become sensitive to His voice and sensitive to His direction for our life.

As a child I can remember my parents always kneeling before God and communing with Him as soon as their feet hit the floor in the mornings. My parents knew that kneeling and praying before God day and night was a necessity. Regardless of what situation they were facing or how they may have felt, they knew it was essential that they face God before they faced their day. Even today at the age of 75 and battling numerous medical conditions, my mother continues to get on her knees and go before God in prayer every morning and every night thanking Him for her family, the blessings He has bestowed upon her and asking for His protection. Spending time with God is one of the greatest privileges to being a Christian.

Relationship with our Heavenly father is essential for our Christian growth. Genesis 1:26 says that we were made in the image of God, referring to our body. We have the responsibility to allow our inner man to be transformed into His image as well; but this will only come through true communion and fellowship with our Heavenly Father. Matthew 7:16 says that we are known by our fruits, referring to our character. Have you noticed that the more time you spend in the presence of people, the more you begin to know, speak and act like them? There are married couples, siblings and friends who spend so much time together that they know what the other is thinking before they even speak. These relationships are built through spending time relating and communing with one another. God wants His daughters to know His mind, His thoughts, and portray His inward image through their lives. The more time we spend in God's presence the more we will know the mind of God for every situation we face in life.

Our God is all knowing and He loves His daughters. He knows everything we will encounter when we walk out of our homes and face the world and wants us to be victorious in every situation. God wants to give us the answers to life. He wants to prepare us for what's ahead and give us inside information on how to be successful, prosperous and victorious.

Most of us will not spend our life in the temple as Anna did, but we are still required to spend personal time with God so we can know Him and His plans for our lives. Isaiah 55:6 says that we are to "Seek the Lord while He may be found, Call upon Him while He is near." Daughters of God; don't take the opportunity to fellowship and commune with God for granted. When we diligently seek His face and His direction we will find that our entire day goes better. If we as the daughters of God never take the time to commune with Him we will miss out on the most important relationship of our life and the one from whom all victories come. No matter how busy you think your day is, you should never be too busy to spend time with the Father.

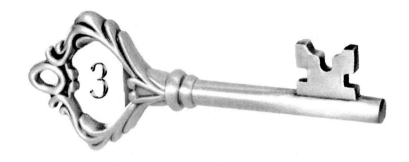

Seek God's Favor

For whoever finds me finds life, and obtains favor from the Lord.
Proverbs 8:35

The next lesson to victorious living is learned from a well-known woman within the Bible: Queen Esther. Most of us have read the story of Queen Esther and know how she went from losing both her parents to being elevated to a Queen. Esther's life teaches us many lessons to becoming victorious. After Queen Vashti was dethroned for insubordination, King Ahasuerus was in search of a new Queen to sit on the royal throne. A notice was sent out to all providences of the kingdom to gather all of the fair young virgins to be brought to the palace for selection of a new Queen. All of the young women brought to the palace were entrusted into the hands of Hegai, the king's chamberlain and keeper of the women. Mordecai, Esther's guardian, brought her to the palace to be presented before the king. Esther immediately gained Hegai's favor, as we see in Esther 2:9:

Now the young woman pleased him, and she obtained his favor; so he readily gave beauty preparations to her, besides her allowance. Then seven choice maidservants were provided for her from the king's palace, and he moved her and her maidservants to the best place in the house of the women.

The first lesson we learn from Esther is that we as daughters of God should seek the favor of God. When we have the favor of God, He grants unto us favor with men. Hegai did not personally know Esther from any of the other young women yet he favored her above all others. It was through this favor that Esther obtained from Hegai the best of everything needed for her preparation to go before the King. Even before the competition began Hegai had already selected Esther as his favorite and began to give her the upper hand in winning the position of Queen, she was appointed the best maids, was assigned to the best place in the palace and was given more than her allotted share of the supplies she would need for the preparation process.

Daughters of God, when you have the favor of God on your life He gives you favor with everyone else you will need favor with to get to where He is leading you. We must seek the favor of God for everything we set out to do for without His favor we will not be victorious.

I remember a time immediately after graduating nursing school that I applied for my first job. After submitting my application to the clerk at a local hospital, a Psychiatric Nurse Manager walked into the office and the clerical person asked her if she had any job openings on the Psychiatric unit. The Nurse Manager replied that there were not any openings at that time. The clerical person who had never met me prior to that day didn't stop there but continued inquiring of the Nurse Manager stating "surely you can use Brenda somewhere even if it's on an as needed basis."

I was sitting there quietly only observing what was going on because this clerical person was speaking up for me as though she were helping a friend. Finally the Nurse Manager stated, "Well, yes, I can put her on the as needed schedule but there is no guarantee of hours." I accepted the position and was immediately hired to the Psychiatric unit as a Registered Nurse. I began working and was offered a full time position on my first day. When you have the favor of God over your life people who don't even know you will speak highly of you and make recommendations under the unction of the spirit of God. The favor of God will give you favor with men in high places and open doors for you that you could never open alone.

When the favor of God is with you, He not only gives you the favor needed with men to work on your behalf, but He also fights through others against those who fight against His plans for your life. In Esther 3 we meet Haman. Haman was the Chief Prince who had a personal hatred towards the Jews, which Queen Esther was. When Haman set out to destroy the Jews he had no idea that he would also be destroying Queen Esther.

There are some people in our life whose plan is not against us personally. They don't even know that we are included in the category of people they hate. Haman's underhanded tactics to destroy the Jews backfired on him after the King discovers that he has plotted to destroy his Queen's people. In Esther 7:9-10, Haman faces his punishment: the King orders that he be hung from the very gallows he made to hang Mordeci, Esther's uncle.

Just as Esther encountered Haman, we will encounter people on our life's journey whose mission is to hinder us from getting to the places God is leading us to; people who set as their primary mission to prove that you are not the right person for the position in which God put you. How many of you have had a person on your job whether ministry or career who seemed out to get you? Women of God, I can declare that when the favor of God is upon you, your "haters" are in danger for the plans they had for your destruction will always backfire on them.

When you have the favor of God He will deal with the "haters" in your life just as He dealt with Haman on Esther's behalf. Daughters of God, we should not worry about those who seek to destroy us or hinder us from fulfilling our God given duties. Our Heavenly Father will deal with those who are against us as long as we are walking in His divine favor.

You may wonder, "How do I gain God's favor?" The only way to obtain the God's favor is to trust Him and walk in obedience to His Word. When we as God's daughters walk in obedience to His directives towards us, God's favor will enable us to stand humbly before great Kings.

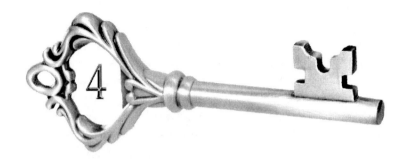

Know Your Purpose

*There are many plans in a man's heart; Nevertheless the Lord's counsel—
that will stand.* **Proverbs 19:21**

In Esther 4, Mordecai notified Queen Esther of the decree sent out by Haman to destroy the Jews. He also sent directives to Esther on what she must do to intercede on behalf of her people. Esther's initial response was like many of ours when we are directed to do something outside of our comfort zones: she began to look at the obstacles. "Everyone knows that no one is allowed to enter into the King's inner courts without being invited or they may be put to death," Esther said, "and I have not been called these thirty days." Esther no doubt had been told the story of Vashti and how she disobeyed the King's order and was dethroned to shame. We can understand her not wanting to walk in Vashti's footsteps of disobedience.

In Esther 4:13-14, Mordecai brought Esther into harsh reality of her current situation, "Do not think in your heart that you will escape in the king's palace any more than all the other Jews. For if you remain completely silent at this time, relief and deliverance will arise for the Jews from another place, but you and your father's house will perish." Mordecai then enlightened Esther further, "Yet who knows whether you have come to the kingdom for such a time as this?"

This leads us to our next key to victorious living for women of God: the importance of knowing your purpose. Esther accepted the responsibility by putting her life on the line to fulfill her obligation to the Jewish people and sends these words to her guardian Mordecai in Esther 4:16, "Go, gather all the Jews who are present in Shushan, and fast for me; neither eat nor drink for three days, night or day My maids and I will fast likewise. And so I will go to the king, which is against the law; and if I perish, I perish!" Esther accepted the challenge of entering into the King's inner courts and, as we read in the scriptures, she found favor in his sight, was welcomed into the inner courts and eventually convinced the King to overturn Haman's decree to have all Jews killed. Esther put her life on the line to fulfill the purpose God had assigned her to do. She recognized, as many of us have, that unless we fulfill God's ordained calling upon us, our life would not be worth living.

Daughters of God, wherever you are in life, I encourage you to seek God to understand the purpose of you being there. God did not put you where you are without reason. God has ordained each of us to fulfill our God-given assignments. As Mordecai told Esther, if you refuse to fulfill your assignments, God will assign it to another person. You don't want to miss out on what God has planned for you.

The danger of not fulfilling your assignments is that you also miss the blessings tied to them. Note that after Esther went before the King on the Jews behalf, he gave her Haman's house as her own. What blessings have you missed out on due to your failure to fulfill a God given assignment in its season? What blessings have your fears hindered you from entering into?

Your assignment may not have been to save the Jewish people it may have been to witness and save the soul you passed by in the supermarket. It may have been to witness of Christ's love to your co-worker or neighbor. Just as Esther saved the Jews, we are responsible for saving lost souls from hell. It may be fearful at times but as God gave Esther favor to fulfill purpose He will give it to you also. I have heard many believers say concerning evangelism, "I can't talk about God at work or I might lose my job." We let all these excuses and fears stop us from fulfilling purpose. Esther had to break the rules to save the Jews; but she was willing to put her life on the line to save her people. What are you willing to put on the line to fulfill your God given assignments?

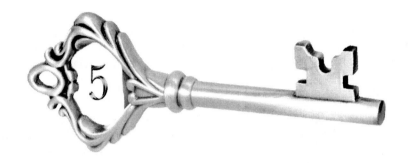

Recognize the Greater Cause:
"It's Not About You"

But Jesus called them to Himself and said to them, "You know that those who are considered rulers over the Gentiles lord it over them, and their great ones exercise authority over them. Yet it shall not be so among you; but whoever desires to become great among you shall be your servant. And whoever of you desires to be first shall be slave of all. For even the Son of Man did not come to be served, but to serve, and to give His life a ransom for many." **Mark 10:42-45**

God had placed Esther in a strategic position of favor with the King to be a voice that he would listen to. Esther was the Queen and she probably thought that God had blessed her to that position for herself alone. Mordecai enlightened her to the probability that maybe God's purpose for your being appointed Queen is not for you alone but for the purpose of saving your people from destruction. Whenever God raises us up—whether through promotion or increase—it is not just for our benefit. Our promotions in life are always tied to the responsibility of helping someone else. We cannot afford to be selfish with the blessings that God has bestowed upon us; rather we should look around our circle of influence to see whom we can bless. Luke 12:48 says, "For everyone to whom much is given, from him much will be required; and to whom much has been committed, of him they will ask the more."

I remember how Princess Diana of the royal family in England was always reaching down from her royal throne to help others. She could have just sat back and allowed others to serve her but her heart for people would not allow her to do that. She understood her position was about helping others. Leadership is not about being put on a pedestal and honored. It is not about how many people we have under our command. It's truly about how many people we serve and how many lives we touch.

As God has promoted me to various positions within my career, there have always been opportunities for me to help others. There have been times when members of my management team would have intentions to treat certain employees unfairly due to their personal prejudices but God put me in a strategic position to speak up on behalf of those who could have been mistreated. God allowed my voice to be heard and granted me with the favor to speak up for others. In each position, God not only fulfilled my selfish ambitions but put me in a position to help others.

I remember one specific situation where I was in a meeting with my management team and an employee was being treated unfairly. God gave me the courage to speak up for righteousness on the person's behalf even when other managers on my team were siding with the wrong. To this day that employee has not forgotten that I spoke up on her behalf. Remember that you are a voice for those who cannot or will not be heard.

As you consider the position that Christ has placed you in during this season of your life be aware of those whom He has called you to serve; to speak up for and to assist in getting them to their next level.

Always remember that regardless of the position you are in and how hard you've worked to get there; the glory goes to God and our ultimate responsibility is to serve others. It's not about us.

Stay Focused on Your Goals

Commit your works to the Lord, and your thoughts will be established.
Proverbs 16:3

Now it happened on the third day that Esther put on her royal robes and stood in the inner court of the king's palace, across from the king's house, while the king sat on his royal throne in the royal house, facing the entrance of the house. So it was, when the king saw Queen Esther standing in the court, that she found favor in his sight, and the king held out to Esther the golden scepter that was in his hand. Then Esther went near and touched the top of the scepter. And the king said to her, "What do you wish, Queen Esther? What is your request? It shall be given to you—up to half the kingdom!" So Esther answered, "If it pleases the king, let the king and Haman come today to the banquet that I have prepared for him." Esther 5:1-4

As Esther stood before the king she was diligent to stay focused on the task at hand, saving her people. King Ahasuerus asked Esther about her request and offered her up to half of his kingdom. Esther did not allow his offer to sway her away from her assignment but requested only to have he and Haman attend a banquet that she would prepare for them. In this action, she demonstrated our next key to victorious living: the ability to stay focused on your goals.

So many of us stray from fulfilling our goals due to other things clouding our vision or distracting us. To appreciate what Esther denied, we must understand that King Ahasuerus reigned over all of the territory from India to Ethiopia, more than 127 provinces. Many of us would have lost focus of our goal and accepted the offer if we had been in Esther's position. However, Esther knew why she was before the king: she was on an assignment. At that point, nothing else mattered.

As women of God we must learn to stay focused on the goals that are set before us. The enemy (Satan) will always bring distractions to deter us from getting to the place that God is leading us to and those distractions can come in many disguises that we all encounter daily.

As I began writing this book, one of the biggest hindrances for me was my love for the television show *Law and Order*. I could sit and watch the marathons all day and realize at the end of the day that I had not completed any notes or chapters for this book. I had to realize that nothing was worth more to me than fulfilling God's calling of my writing. I had my cable disconnected and began using an antenna, which limited my ability to watch my favorite shows. Although this may seem drastic for some, it was well worth it for me because it enabled me to focus on my God-given assignments.

Satan's job is to hinder us from accomplishing our God-given assignments. Distractions are sent to have us erroneously believe that the determent is of more value than our assignment. I have witnessed ministers who were committed to God and doing His work become sidetracked when they marry, have children or get a promotion. The first thing that we as believers must understand is that God will not send anything in our lives that would deter us from fulfilling our calling; not even temporarily. If He sends you a spouse, child or promotion, it should enhance your fulfillment of purpose not decrease it.

To be clear, I am not saying that family should not change your time management, but laying aside your God-given assignments should not be an option. I have witnessed believers acquire promotions on their jobs and think just because promotion is a good thing it was a God thing. That very promotion took them out of church and fellowship with like believers and ended up being a decoy of the enemy to get them out of God's will with what seemed to them at the time to be justifiable cause.

Esther could have sold out on making her request of the King on behalf of Jews and settled for half the kingdom. Acquiring half the kingdom under King Ahaseurus would have been a great accomplishment for a woman; but it was not her goal. Fulfilling your God-given assignments must be so important to you that nothing else matters. When you put your God-given assignments first in your life God will always grant unto you the desires of your heart.

Esther didn't get half the kingdom but let's look at what she did acquire.

- She no longer had to hide the fact that she was a Jew from the King

- Her Uncle Mordecai's life was spared and he became second only to King Ahasueres in the kingdom

- She saved the Jews from annihilation

- She no longer feared going before the King uninvited.

- She knew that she had a voice the King would listen to

As you can see, what Esther acquired was far greater than half a kingdom. What distractions have been set before you that are hindering your fulfilling your God-given assignments? Whatever your response to that question; you must make the decision as to how you will handle the distractions. When your God-given assignments become so important to you that you are willing to make the necessary changes in your life to accomplish them, you will see as Esther did that it will be well worth the sacrifice.

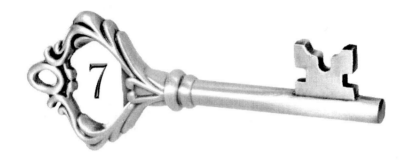

Be Faithful Over Your Responsibilities

His lord said to him, "Well done, good and faithful servant; you have been faithful over a few things, I will make you ruler over many things. Enter into the joy of your lord." Matthew 25:23

Rebecca, the woman selected to be Isaac's wife, demonstrates the next key to becoming a victorious woman: be faithful over your responsibilities. Being faithful refers to our level of accountability, reliability and trustworthiness. Victorious women know the importance of being where they are supposed to be when they are supposed to be there.

In Genesis 24 Abraham directed his servant to go to his home country of Mesopotamia to find a suitable wife for his son Isaac. The servant went to the land of Abraham's family and stopped at a well outside the city at a time when the women were due to come out and draw water. Timing and location were important factors in the servant's success: He first had to know where to find the woman and then he had to be in the location at the right time. Since women were responsible for going to the well daily to draw water, he knew the well was a good place to find Isaac's future wife. In Genesis 24:11-15, Abraham's servant prays for God's favor in finding Isaac's wife:

And he made his camels kneel down outside the city by a well of water at evening time, the time when women go out to draw water. Then he said, "O Lord God of my master Abraham, please give me success this day, and show kindness to my master Abraham. Behold, here I stand by the well of water, and the daughters of the men of the city are coming out to draw water. Now let it be that the young woman to whom I say, 'Please let down your pitcher that I may drink,' and she says, 'Drink, and I will also give your camels a drink'—let her be the one You have appointed for Your servant Isaac. And by this I will know that You have shown kindness to my master." And it happened, before he had finished speaking, that behold, Rebekah, who was born to Bethuel, son of Milcah, the wife of Nahor, Abraham's brother, came out with her pitcher on her shoulder.

Unknown to her, Rebecca had a divine appointment set by God and she reported for duty on time. So often we as women have a tendency to miss divine appointments because we aren't in the assigned or appointed locations at the right time. Rebecca was the first woman to arrive at the well after the servant prayed, showing her diligence to fulfill her assigned duties.

I encounter women daily who take punctuality for granted. They think it is acceptable to be a few minutes tardy; this was not so for Rebecca. Abraham's servant thought it was important to meet the woman at the place where her attitude towards fulfilling responsibilities could be assessed. A person's level of diligence to fulfill assigned tasks is a reflection of their readiness to be elevated to their next level. Going to the well on a daily basis to draw water was a chore assigned to Rebecca and she did it faithfully.

As a child, my siblings and I were given chores such as washing dishes, sweeping, mopping, etc. These were not fun tasks but they had to be done; if we did not complete them, we were punished. On one occasion, my father had traveled out of state for a week to visit his family and left my two brothers in charge of watering the cattle. My brothers were young at the time but quite capable of fulfilling the task. Upon my father's return, he noted that the cows were dehydrated and the trough for watering the cattle was dry. The boys had not fulfilled their responsibility and it could have cost my father the loss of many cattle. The boys were punished and my father saw that they were not ready to accept that level of responsibility.

Being Isaac's wife was a big responsibility for a woman to assume. A thorough assessment of how this woman handled her current responsibilities was a reflection of how she would handle future responsibilities. If we as women cannot diligently manage our current responsibilities then we are not ready for the next level. Although it was only drawing water from the well, Rebecca took her responsibility serious and did it cheerfully. When you are diligent to faithfully fulfill the duties currently assigned to you then promotion is sure to follow. Rebecca's diligence in fulfilling small responsibilities led her to acquiring the best promotion of her life. She didn't know that she was being observed by Abraham's servant in consideration of becoming Isaac's wife; she only knew that she had a job to do. Had Rebecca waited and been the last to come to the well that evening Abraham's servant may have chosen another beautiful woman for Isaac in her absence.

As a Manager, I always take note of those employees who take their responsibilities seriously. When an opportunity for promotion arises, they are the ones I recommend. I can't promote a person who is not diligent about their current responsibilities, as they would not be an example for others to follow. Daughters of God; what responsibilities have you been assigned? How many times have you become lax in the performance of your assigned duties?

Some of you may never know what opportunities you may have missed due to your lack of accountability and not being in your assigned location at the appointed time. The good thing is that you can make the change today to become diligent concerning fulfilling your responsibilities. Some of the missed opportunities will never return to you but you can make up your mind to not miss another. God is a forgiving Father and regardless of where you currently are He still has great things planned for your life. You now have to make up your mind to be diligent in fulfilling your responsibilities and obligations.

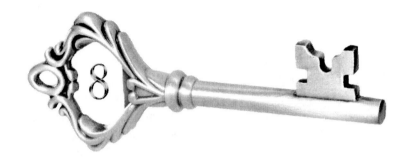

Develop a Servant's Heart

So when He had washed their feet, taken His garments, and sat down again, He said to them, "Do you know what I have done to you? You call Me Teacher and Lord, and you say well, for so I am. If I then, your Lord and Teacher, have washed your feet, you also ought to wash one another's feet. John 13:12-14

Rebecca also demonstrated our next key to becoming a victorious woman: develop a servant's heart.

Now let it be that the young woman to whom I say, 'Please let down your pitcher that I may drink,' and she says, 'Drink, and I will also give your camels a drink'—let her be the one You have appointed for Your servant Isaac. And by this I will know that You have shown kindness to my master." And it happened, before he had finished speaking, that behold, Rebekah, who was born to Bethuel, son of Milcah, the wife of Nahor, Abraham's brother, came out with her pitcher on her shoulder. Now the young woman was very beautiful to behold, a virgin; no man had known her. And she went down to the well, filled her pitcher, and came up. And the servant ran to meet her and said, "Please let me drink a little water from your pitcher." So she said, "Drink, my lord." Then she quickly let her pitcher down to her hand, and gave him a drink. Genesis 24: 14-18

Isn't it interesting that one of the characteristics that Abraham's servant looked for in a wife for Isaac was that she has the heart of a servant? A servant is defined by The Free Dictionary (2003 – 2015) as "one who expresses submission, recognizance, or debt to another". The expression of submission or servitude does not make us any less a woman; rather, it expresses our ability to esteem others. Rebecca's submission towards Abraham's servant demonstrated her ability to be submissive towards her husband as his helpmate. Rebecca was not indebted to Abraham's servant nor did she know who he was. She responded with what was already in her heart: a reverence of others. It is so important that we incorporate this important characteristic into our everyday living whether married or single.

As single women, you never know who may be watching you and considering you as a wife. As women, we often hear about our responsibility to submit to our husbands, but the heart of submission should not wait until you get married. Your ability to submit should be incorporated into your everyday lifestyle. God places people around us daily whom we can serve. It should be demonstrated to your family, toward your friends, on your job and wherever you are assigned. Daughters of God, when was the last time you served someone else when it was not mandated? In Luke 22:27 Jesus asked His disciples, "For who is greater, he who sits at the table, or he who serves? Is it not he who sits at the table? Yet I am among you as the One who serves." The ability to humbly serve others is not a sign of weakness but an indication of one's strength. It takes more for a person to serve another than it takes to be served. Any woman can be the recipient of service but it takes genuine humility to serve another without mandate.

In Genesis 24:59 and 61 as Rebecca was preparing to leave her family she was sent away with her very own maids. When you have a servant's heart towards others you will gain reverence in return. Just as anything else in the kingdom of God, we reap what we sow. Rebecca served others and she was served in return. Women of God let me encourage you to always seek opportunities to serve others.

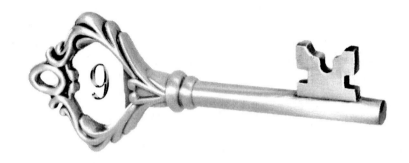

Go Above and Beyond Expectations

And whatever you do, do it heartily, as to the Lord and not to men, knowing that from the Lord you will receive the reward of the inheritance; for you serve the Lord Christ. **Colossians 3:23-24**

After Abraham's servant asked Rebecca for a drink of water, Rebecca lowered her pitcher and replied, "Drink my Lord." She then saw that his camels were also in need of water and drew them water. She proceeded to run back and forth, refilling the trough, until all 10 camels had enough to drink. In doing this, Rebecca demonstrated the next key to becoming a victorious woman: the willingness to go above and beyond expectations.

There is something great to be said of a woman who goes above and beyond the call of duty. Rebecca could have merely fulfilled the servant's request for water, but she identified that the camels needed water also, and didn't wait to be asked before she volunteered to water them. As daughters of God we too must be willing to go above and beyond the call of duty when we see needs.

As a manager, I have seen many employees only doing enough to meet the minimum requirements of their job duties when they were aware of other needs. I have also had employees who cared enough about their job and the success of the company to learn not only their duties but the duties of others around them. These employees do not wait to be asked to do something but identify needs and get the job done. As I mentioned earlier, these employees are the ones who receive my vote when the opportunity for promotion and pay increase arises.

In Corporate America, people have become obsessed with the "what's in it for me" mentality as opposed to going the extra mile without demand or expectations. Rebecca's heart was towards ensuring that the needs of Abraham's servant were met. She didn't stop filling that trough until all 10 camels were satisfied. That's a lot of running back and forth! Rebecca got the job done and Abraham's servant took notes of her generosity. In Geneses 24:22, Rebecca is rewarded for her service: Abraham's servant gives her a golden nose ring weighing half a shekel and two bracelets for her wrists weighing ten shekels of gold. What a reward, especially considering she was serving from the goodness of her heart with no expectations.

As women of God we must ensure that whatever we do for others comes from a pure heart without expectations of anything in return. Though you shouldn't expect anything, it is important to note that what you do for others always comes back to you in some way. Colossians 3:23-24 says, "And whatsoever ye do, do it heartily, as to the Lord, and not unto men; knowing that of the Lord ye shall receive the reward of the inheritance: for ye serve the Lord Christ."

Rebecca's service towards Abraham's servant came from her pure heart, not with an expectation of getting anything in return. As the story goes on, Rebecca gets more than she ever dreamed of receiving: She was connected to the wealthiest man on earth. Women of God, whomever you have opportunity to serve, serve as unto the Lord, knowing that when you serve from a pure heart you will receive a Godly reward.

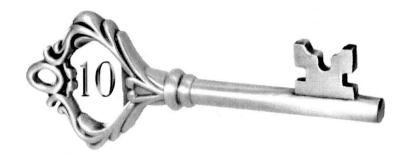

Be Hospitable Toward Others

Do not forget to entertain strangers, for by so doing some have unwittingly entertained angels. **Hebrews 13:2**

The next characteristic demonstrated by Rebecca that will aid in our victory is the ability to be warm, generous and hospitable towards others. As noted in her initial meeting of Abraham's servant after providing for his need of water for him and his camels, Rebecca's hospitality didn't stop there. When asked if her Father had room for their lodging, Rebecca replied in Genesis 24:25, "We have both straw and feed enough, and room to lodge." Hospitality has almost become extinct in our society. People have become so focused on themselves and their needs that they don't have time to look after the cares of others. This was not the case with Rebecca, who welcomingly invited the strangers back to her family's home.

As daughters of God, we should always ensure that we are hospitable toward others, both friends and strangers. Hebrews 13:2 says, "Do not forget to entertain strangers, for by so doing some have unwittingly entertained angels." Rebecca had no idea that she was serving the servant of the wealthiest man on earth, nor did she know his reason for being in town. Her hospitable nature was a part of who she was. True hospitality should be demonstrated consistently in our actions. Being hospitable makes others feel welcomed and accepted. As women our goal should be going the extra mile and doing for others what we would want done for us if we were the strangers in town.

As Rebecca opened her home to the servant she had passed the test and demonstrated all the characteristics the servant was looking for in a wife for Isaac. After Rebecca opened the doors to their home for lodging, the servant bowed his head and began to worship God; for he had found the wife for Isaac.

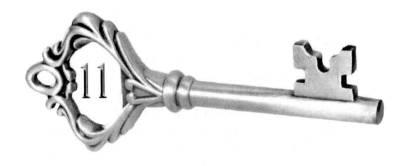

When Opportunity Knocks, Don't Delay

I returned and saw under the sun that—The race is not to the swift, Nor the battle to the strong, Nor bread to the wise, Nor riches to men of understanding, Nor favor to men of skill; But time and chance happen to them all. **Ecclesiastes 9:11**

Upon entering the home, Abraham's servant told Rebecca's family the reason he was in town—to find a wife for his servant's son—and that Rebecca had been confirmed by God to be the one. The servant awoke the next morning ready to return home with Rebecca, only to find that her family was not ready to let her go and requested that she remain with them an additional ten days before leaving. The servant insisted on leaving promptly with Rebecca to return to his master. When approached and asked what she wished to do, Rebecca's answer was, "I will go." Wow! Talk about your life changing at the blink of an eye. Rebecca did not delay; she was ready to embrace the new opportunity that was before her. Although I am sure that she loved her family and they loved her, she knew a new season was upon her and she embraced it.

Many times I have witnessed women with the opportunity of a lifetime before them who turn it down because of fear of leaving their comfort zone. They turn down new job opportunities, new relationships, travel opportunities, scholarships to school, stepping out into their own businesses and so much more because they have become comfortable in their present situation and feel safe there.

Rebecca left her family and everything she knew to marry a man she had never met.

As aspiring victorious women, we must pray and ask God daily to help us to recognize the opportunities that He sets before us. Do not delay opportunities by procrastinating or finding an excuse not to walk through an open door. Rebecca had spent her entire lifetime enjoying her family. I imagine that like every young woman Rebecca had desires to marry and have a family. When that opportunity was before her and she had to make the decision as to whether to go or procrastinate, she was ready for the change.

What opportunities are knocking at your door? How will you respond? Will you find a reason not to move forward or will you walk boldly through that open door? Daughters of God, I pray that you don't miss out on the divine opportunities for a better life sent divinely to you by God. My prayer is that you recognize the times and the seasons of your life when divine opportunities knock, and that you reply as Rebecca did: "I will go."

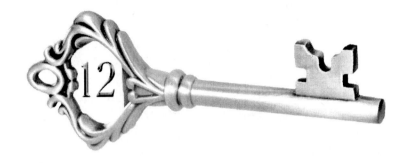

Be a Woman of Your Word

If a man makes a vow to the Lord, or swears an oath to bind himself by some agreement, he shall not break his word; he shall do according to all that proceeds out of his mouth. Numbers 30:2

Our Heavenly Father stands behind every word He speaks; this is one of the characteristics of God that makes Him reliable and gives us the faith to trust every word that proceeds from his mouth. Just as our Heavenly Father is a God of His Word, we as His daughters are to follow in His footsteps. In Numbers 23:19, Balaam proclaimed, "God is not a man, that He should lie, nor a son of man, that He should repent. Has He said, and will He not do? Or has He spoken, and will He not make it good?" As the daughters of God, we too should demonstrate this trait of being women who stand behind our words. Fulfilling our words gives us credibility with others and it makes our Heavenly Father proud.

In 1 Samuel chapters 1-2 we learn about Hannah, who demonstrated standing by her word regardless of the cost. Hannah was barren. She was married to Elkanah, who also had another wife, Pininah, who had many children. During the annual time for making sacrifices to the Lord at Shiloh, Hannah was miserable because of the teasing from her adversary of her being barren. While bitter and weeping in anger, Hannah prayed in her heart to the Lord and asked for a male child. She made a vow to the Lord that if He would bless her with a male child she would give him back to the Lord all the days of his life. In I Samuel 1:17, Eli the priest sealed her request by telling her to, "Go in peace, and the God of Israel grant your petition which you have asked of Him." Hannah was no longer saddened but went her way and ate.

In I Samuel 1:19, we see the fulfillment of Hannah's prayer: God granted to her a male child. Hannah then cared for the child until he was weaned, after which she fulfilled her vow to God and presents her only son Samuel to Eli the Priest:

Now when she had weaned him, she took him up with her, with three bulls, one ephah of flour, and a skin of wine, and brought him to the house of the Lord in Shiloh. And the child was young. Then they slaughtered a bull, and brought the child to Eli. And she said, "O my lord! As your soul lives, my lord, I am the woman who stood by you here, praying to the Lord. For this child I prayed, and the Lord has granted me my petition which I asked of Him. Therefore I also have lent him to the Lord; as long as he lives he shall be lent to the Lord." So they worshiped the Lord there. 1 Samuel 1:24-27

Hannah gave her only son to God just as she had promised, demonstrating one of the most important characteristics of any victorious woman: to be a woman of your word regardless of the cost. How many promises have you made to others but failed to fulfill? Sometimes we make promises to others out of emotions or just out of the blue without thinking through the cost of that promise.

There was a time I would notice myself making promises to do things for others, such as bake a cake or cook a dish, only to realize that time had passed and I had not delivered on the promise. I had good intentions to fulfill the promise; however, for one reason or another, I didn't. Though the reasons felt valid at the time, the fact is I didn't keep my word and let others down. As daughters of God, our word should be our bond. It is very important that we consider the cost of any promise we make to others. We must get into the habit of thinking before we speak and counting the cost of our promises prior to making them.

In churches, I have witnessed countless parents stand and dedicate or give back their child to God. I wonder whether these well intending parents actually know what giving the child back to God really means or if this is only a humble gesture. What would be their response if God called that child to the mission field at the age of 12? Would they obediently hand the child over or would they tell God that he/she is not old enough? Ecclesiastes 5:4-5 says, "When you make a vow to God, do not delay to pay it; for he has no pleasure in fools. Pay what you have vowed—Better not to vow than to vow and not pay."

God places value on us fulfilling our vows and He demonstrates this by being a God who always keeps His Word. If our Heavenly Father did not keep His Word to us, how would we feel? For most of us, there would be a loss of credibility and we would lose trust in Him. Even if His intentions were to fulfill the vow at the time of the promise, we will question every promise thereafter. Well, that's the way others feel when we don't keep our word to them, untrustworthy and after that they begin to doubt our intentions and any further words we speak. Our Heavenly Father watches over His Word to perform it (Jeremiah 1:12). As daughters of God we should walk accordingly.

Hannah had only one son at the time, but she was mindful of the vow she had made before God. I know that sometimes things in our life don't go as planned and we just cannot fulfill a vow: What do we do in those cases? According to James 4:15, when we are making our plans to do something we should say, "If the Lord wills, we shall do this or do that," and we should put forth every natural effort to fulfill the vow unless God says otherwise. When things happen that hinder us from fulfilling the promise, we should face the person we made the vow to, explain our current situation as to why we cannot fulfill the vow and apologize. Now, if the opportunity does present itself where the vow can be fulfilled then by all means do so.

As you strive to become a woman of your word you will begin to consider cautiously the words and vows that proceed out of your mouth and gain credibility with others. Daughters of God, I urge you to take a moment to consider if there have been any vows or obligations that you have made to others and did not follow through on fulfilling. I now challenge you to make it right by fulfilling that vow regardless of the number of years, months or days that have passed. I can guarantee you the person you gave your word to has not forgotten. As you take the responsibility to fulfilling your word, you will begin to consider the cost of the commitments you make to others and be well on your way to becoming a woman of your word.

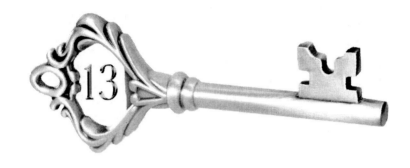

Learn to Celebrate Others' Blessings

*Rejoice with those who rejoice...*Romans 12:15

As we study the scriptures about Elizabeth, the mother of John the Baptist, she teaches us our next key to victory: the ability to celebrate others' blessings. Although Elizabeth was pregnant with her first child after being labeled barren, she openly celebrated and honored the blessing of Mary, the mother of Jesus. Elizabeth herself was experiencing the joy of a long-awaited, miraculous pregnancy but she became overjoyed when Mary, the mother of her Savior, came into her home and exalted the miracle of Mary in her salutation:

And it happened, when Elizabeth heard the greeting of Mary, that the babe leaped in her womb; and Elizabeth was filled with the Holy Spirit. Then she spoke out with a loud voice and said, "Blessed are you among women, and blessed is the fruit of your womb! But why is this granted to me, that the mother of my Lord should come to me? For indeed, as soon as the voice of your greeting sounded in my ears, the babe leaped in my womb for joy. Blessed is she who believed, for there will be a fulfillment of those things which were told her from the Lord." Luke 1: 41

Notice that the first word out of Elizabeth's mouth was not the tooting of her own horn and announcement of her own pregnancy, but it was in celebration of Mary being the "Mother of my Lord." In life we can become so consumed by our own accomplishments that we neglect the opportunity to celebrate the blessings of our fellow sisters. Elizabeth was genuine in her honor of Mary and counted it a privilege to be in her presence. Every woman loves to be amongst those who celebrate her. You will notice in Luke 1:56 that Mary resided with Elizabeth three months before returning home. It is nurturing and reassuring to be in the presence of those who see you as blessed and can celebrate your blessings, your calling and you, as a person. We all need a friend who can genuinely celebrate our successes and blessings.

Have you ever been in a situation where you were experiencing a blessing or success and the person you shared it with was so consumed with their own issues that she didn't take the time to listen and celebrate with you? I have, and it is definitely not a good feeling. You soon become less willing to be in that person's presence or share your future good news with them.

As daughters of God we must learn to celebrate one another's blessings and accomplishments. It is so easy to allow jealousy and envy to slip into our hearts when we see a fellow sister with something that we lack or being promoted (whether spiritually or naturally) to levels greater than ours. We must remember that our Heavenly Father is not a respecter of persons. He will do for us what He has done for our sisters if we ask and seek to please Him in all that we do.

This is not free reign to say, "Well you did it for her, Lord." When asking God for things we must have pure hearts and righteous motives. Our motive must not be asking for something just to be "better" in our own eyes than someone else. You will never truly be satisfied when you are measuring your success and desires against what another person possesses. Spiritual maturity is reflected in your ability to not be intimidated by the successes of others.

Just as Elizabeth celebrated and rejoiced with Mary, we learn in Luke 1:58 that when her neighbors and family heard how the Lord had shown mercy to her (Elizabeth) they rejoiced with her when she gave birth to her son John. When you can celebrate and rejoice with others, God will direct others to celebrate with you.

When was the last time you rejoiced and celebrated someone else's blessings and successes? When I hear of a fellow sister being blessed with her long-awaited mate or pregnancy, my heart wants to be a blessing to them. As a single woman, I may still be waiting for my husband and children, but I know that when I can celebrate with my sisters they will celebrate with me.

I was not always like this. There was a time in my earlier single years that when others were blessed with their mates that I cried out to God and asked "Lord when is mine coming, I have been waiting for so long?" This negative, selfish attitude hindered my ability to truly celebrate with my sisters. I would even judge my fellow sisters as being not as good as me and somehow considered myself more worthy of the blessing than them. Thank God for deliverance!

49

Daughters of God, I challenge you to always find a reason to celebrate your fellow sisters in Christ. As you mature in this area of your life you open the door for others to celebrate with you. When your time comes you will not have to celebrate alone.

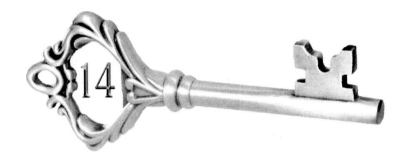

Admit Your Mistakes

Confess your trespasses to one another, and pray for one another, that you may be healed. The effective, fervent prayer of a righteous man avails much. James 5:16

In Genesis 16 Sarai, the wife of Abraham teaches us yet another key to victory that many of us find hard to do: admit our mistakes. We have all read or heard the story of Sarai and Abraham and how they were promised offspring by God. After many years had passed and the promise had not yet been fulfilled, Sarai, who was growing older, decided to take matters into her own hands by having her maidservant, Hagar, bear a child for Abraham. Genesis 16:4 states, "So he went in to Hagar, and she conceived. And when she saw that she had conceived, her mistress became despised in her eyes." After having her maid now looking upon her despitefully, Sarai realized that she had made the biggest mistake of her life and said to her husband Abraham, "My wrong be upon you! I gave my maid into your embrace; and when she saw that she had conceived, I became despised in her eyes. The Lord judge between you and me" (Genesis 16:5). Sarai thought that she had the answer to fulfilling God's promise but her solution ended up smacking her in the face with consequences still being felt around the world today.

As daughters of God we must learn to admit our mistakes. Our ability to admit our wrongs leads us closer to getting things right and aligning ourselves with God's plan. After Sarai admitted to her wrong, she was then given permission by her husband to deal with Hagar. Had Sarai never admitted to the wrong, she would probably have led a miserable life being despised and teased by Hagar, her maidservant.

All of us have made mistakes in our lives and some of those mistakes have cost us dearly. It is only through the recognition and admittance of our mistakes that we can get things right. It takes a brave woman to admit that she was wrong, whether to her husband, children or boss. The longer we delay in admitting to a wrong, the longer the enemy will torment us and hold it over our heads. If we as women of God confess our mistakes and wrongs God is faithful to forgive us and restore us. Notice that Sarai's mistake did not cancel out her promised son; God still fulfilled His Word. Daughters of God, whatever mistakes you have made in your lives, it is never too late to admit the wrong and line your life up with the will of God. Our Heavenly Father is faithful and forgiving and He wants to forgive you. Admitting a mistake does not make you less of a person but opens the door for you to correct the wrong.

Sarai came to the conclusion that although she desired offspring for Abraham, putting up with Hagar's disrespect was not worth it. What have you been putting up with due to a wrong decision? Is it worth the consequences? If not, now is the time to get it right. Don't let another day go by without admitting your wrong. Don't keep putting up with the enemy's torment. I know of women who kept important information from their husband and lived year after year with the fear that he might one day find out. I know children who made mistakes and refused to tell their parents, instead choosing to live in fear that one day their secret would be revealed. Refusing to admit to your mistakes can cost you relationships, marriages, children, job, friends and peace of mind.

Whatever your mistake, it is not worth allowing the enemy to torment you over it. Daughters of God make it a point today to get your life back in line with God's plan by admitting those mistakes that have been hovering over your head for so long, you will feel so much better when you do.

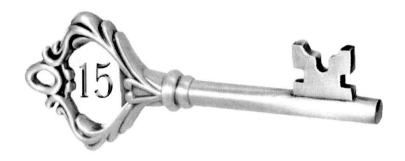

Cultivate a Heart of Humility

When pride comes, then comes shame; but with the humble is wisdom.
Proverbs 11:2

Our next lesson to victory is to cultivate a heart of humility. Humility is defined by Merriam-Webster (2015) as not thinking of your-self as better than other people. I have so often witnessed Christian women who get promotions, a new car, a spouse, etc. only to begin looking down upon their fellow sisters in Christ, some of whom had a hand in helping them to get where they are. As daughters of God, regardless of how far up the success ladder we get we must understand that it is by the grace of God that we are where we are. It is not because we are better than others; it's all by the grace of God.

In Genesis 16, we see the spirit of pride showing its ugly face through Hagar, Sarai's maidservant. After Hagar conceived a child with Abraham, Sarai's husband, she began to despise Sarai (Genesis 16:4). Now we must remember that Sarai is the very person who opened the door to Hagar bearing Abraham's son. Had it not been for Sarai, Hagar would never have had this seemingly great opportunity presented to her. How dare she!

This is a behavior that is seen so frequently today: women become blessed and advance in life only to begin looking down upon others and seeing themselves as better than others. After Sarai admits her mistake to Abraham, he then grants her permission to deal with Hagar. Hagar was pregnant with Abraham's child but Sarai still had his heart and loyalty. Hagar overestimated her role and her value in Abraham's life and had to deal with the consequences of disrespecting Sarai.

And Sarai said unto Abram, My wrong be upon thee: I have given my maid into thy bosom; and when she saw that she had conceived, I was despised in her eyes: the Lord judge between me and thee. But Abram said unto Sarai, Behold, thy maid is in thine hand; do to her as it pleaseth thee. And when Sarai dealt hardly with her, she fled from her face. Genesis 16: 5

Proverbs 16:18 says, "Pride goes before destruction, a haughty spirit before a fall." Hagar was reminded of her place in Abraham's life the hard way. I have seen many women walking in pride; and many have taken great falls and learned humility the hard way. If we maintain a meek and humble spirit before God and others, then we don't have to take the plunge from promotions or decrease in status to learn humbleness. Hagar was in the wilderness crying from Sarai's rebuke when she was visited by an angel of the Lord who directed her in Genesis 16:9 to, "Return to thy mistress, and submit thyself under her hands." Hagar had to rid herself of the pride.

Daughters of God always walk in humility. Never look down upon another person because you have something they don't. Regardless of how high and mighty you are, the same God that lifted you up can also bring you back down. Psalm 25:9 remind us that "The humble He guides in justice, and the humble He teaches His way." Can you imagine the heights of success we would go if we were to always walk with a heart of humility? Daughters of God, I challenge you to examine your life for pride in any areas. If you find any, deal with it before God deals with you.

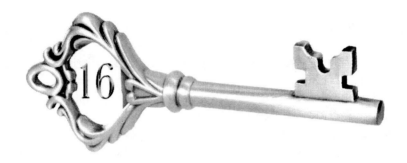

See Beyond Your Nothings

And my God shall supply all your need according to His riches in glory by Christ Jesus. **Philippians 4:19**

In II Kings 4 we are introduced to a widow woman who is about to lose her two sons into slavery to satisfy her debts. Upon her encounter with Elisha she informed him that her deceased husband was a son of the one of the Prophets and feared the Lord. She continued to tell him about the debt she owes and that the creditors were on their way to take away her sons into slavery. The Prophet Elisha questioned her, "What do you have in your house?" To this she replied, "Your maidservant has nothing in the house but a jar of oil" (II Kings 4:2 NKJV). As many of us do when we fall into a crisis situation to which we see no means, the widow woman's first response to Elisha was that she had "nothing." She then quickly interceded with "but a jar of oil," thus leading to our next key to victorious living: the ability to see beyond your nothing.

Elisha then gave the widow woman instructions, "Go, borrow vessels from everywhere, from all your neighbors—empty vessels; do not gather just a few. And when you have come in, you shall shut the door behind you and your sons; then pour it into all those vessels, and set aside the full ones" (II Kings 4:3). We then learn that:

She went from him and shut the door behind her and her sons, who brought the vessels to her; and she poured it out. Now it came to pass, when the vessels were full, that she said to her son, "Bring me another vessel." And he said to her, "There is not another vessel." So the oil ceased. Then she came and told the man of God. And he said, "Go, sell the oil and pay your debt; and you and your sons live on the rest." (II Kings 4:5-7)

Isn't it amazing how God met the widow's need by using something she already possessed?

Many times I have encountered God-gifted women who in their time of need neglect to see the value of the many gifts and treasures that God has placed within them. It is as though when they face a crisis situation and cannot see how the need will be met they lose faith. They become blinded by the enemy and only focus on the things that they don't have, never stopping to consider and take inventory of the many talents, gifts and treasures that our Heavenly Father has placed within them that could be used to meet their need.

Satan's job is to blind us from seeing beyond the nothing of our situations because then and only then can he convince us to give up on God. Satan knows that God always has provisions for His daughters and if we could only see beyond the nothing of our situation we would see the bright future that God has planned for us. As we see with the widow woman, Elisha used something that she already possessed to supply her needs.

Deuteronomy 8:18 (NKJV) says, "And you shall remember the Lord your God, for it is He who gives you power to get wealth, that He may establish His covenant which He swore to your fathers, as it is this day." Our Heavenly Father has put within us everything that we will need to conquer every obstacle that comes our way. As daughters of the living God, our Heavenly Father will never leave us with nothing. Daughters of God never hit rock bottom there is always something in their possession that God can work with.

What current needs do you have in your life to which you see no means to meet? Whatever it is, I will ask you a question similar to what Elisha asked the widow woman: What do you have in your house? What skills, talents and abilities lie within you?

Can you cook? Then maybe you can sell meals or work at a restaurant. Can you sew? Then maybe you can start an alteration business. Whatever skills or abilities you possess someone is always willing to pay for it. Daughters of God, in whatever areas of your life that you have focused on your "nothing," I challenge you to look again and see the exception to the nothing. Whatever the exception to your "nothing," surrender it to God, obey His directives and watch him meet your needs with the very thing you possessed all the time.

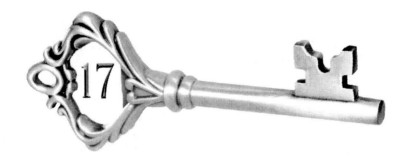

You Can't Tell Everybody Everything

Then Caleb quieted the people before Moses, and said, "Let us go up at once and take possession, for we are well able to overcome it." But the men who had gone up with him said, "We are not able to go up against the people, for they are stronger than we." And they gave the children of Israel a bad report of the land which they had spied out, saying, "The land through which we have gone as spies is a land that devours its inhabitants, and all the people whom we saw in it are men of great stature. There we saw the giants (the descendants of Anak came from the giants); and we were like grasshoppers in our own sight, and so we were in their sight."
Numbers 13:30-33

In II Kings 4 we are introduced to the Shunammite woman who was blessed with a son at the word of Elisha. She was hospitable towards Elisha whenever he would pass through the city. Of her we learn that Elisha the Prophet promised her she would receive a son at a set time the following year. The Shunammite woman received the promised son, who then becomes ill and dies in her lap when he is only a lad. As the mother's spirit became vexed, she laid her son upon a bed and set out to find Elisha. In II Kings 4:22-23 we read, "Then she called to her husband, and said, 'Please send me one of the young men and one of the donkeys, that I may run to the man of God and come back.' So he said, 'Why are you going to him today? It is neither the New Moon nor the Sabbath.' And she said, 'It is well.'" She did not inform her husband that the son has just died; she only said that she must find the man of God. In doing this, she demonstrated our next key to becoming a victorious woman: you can't tell everybody everything.

So many times we as women innocently share too much information with the wrong people thinking that they are of the same mindset as we only to our detriment. The Shunammite woman knew that Elisha could raise her son from the dead; she had faith in the man of God. Who knows what her husband would have said had she informed him that the son was dead? He may have prepared for a funeral and not have had hope that there was a miracle in the making. As the Shunammite woman approached Elisha's camp Gehazi, Elisha's servant, comes out to meet her:

> *And so she departed, and went to the man of God at Mount Carmel. So it was, when the man of God saw her afar off that he said to his servant Gehazi; "Look, the Shunammite woman! Please run now to meet her, and say to her, 'Is it well with you? Is it well with your husband? Is it well with the child?" And she answered, "It is well."* (II Kings 4:25)

Note that when asked she doesn't share the facts of the situation with the man of God's servant; she only shares that "it is well." You may wonder why she continued to say things were well after her son was dead. I believe it is because some people may have called the son's death the end of the matter and encouraged her to deal with it instead of having faith with her that it was not too late for a miracle.

Have you ever believed God for something or had big dreams and shared it with someone only to be discouraged or told that that it would never happen for you. You look for someone who will share in or assist in encouraging you in the matter only to have your dreams or hopes shattered. That is why as daughters of God it is so important we know the people in our life who have like faith and will encourage us in the things we are hoping for. Believe the words that God has spoken over your life and share it only with those who will believe with you. If the Shunammite woman had informed everybody of what was going on with her son he may have been buried before Elisha arrived on the scene and she would have missed her miracle.

How many times have you allowed others to talk you out of something that you truly believed in? You had faith in God, but allowed the opinions of others to cloud your vision and cause you to cease in the pursuit of your dreams. What dreams have you buried because someone who didn't understand your faith talked you out of it? It may have been a career, a business or something you desired to accomplish. Whatever the dream you have buried now is the time to dig it up and breathe life back into it. Get into the company of like believers and encouragers. Notice I said 'like believers.' Not all believers will have the faith to agree with you that your miracle is on the way. Know those who can see and believe with you. In II Kings 4:27, the Shunammite woman told only Elisha of the death of her son. Elisha then went to the woman's house and performed the miracle of raising the son up from the dead.

Daughters of God it is not too late to resurrect your dead dreams. Never allow another person to pull your faith down to their level. God meets each of us at the level of our faith. Just because another believer cannot see or understand what you believe God for does not mean that it is not for you. It only means that you shared it with the wrong person.

Note that Gehazi, Elisha's servant, was given directives on what to do to raise the child but the Shunammite woman refused to go with him and insisted on not leaving without Elisha. It was not that the child could not have been healed through Gehazi's obedience to the man of God; it was that the Shunammite woman's faith was in Elisha performing the miracle. That is why we see that although Gehazi was obedient to Elisha, the son was not raised because the woman's faith was not there. God meets us at our level of faith. You will also notice throughout the New Testament when Jesus performed miracles He did it "according to your faith."

Daughters of God the heavens are the limit to what you can have. If your dreams and desires are approved in the heavens then you can experience and have it here on the earth. On your way to fulfilling those dreams know that the road may not be a smooth one; In II Kings 4:24 the Shunammite woman told her driver, "Drive, and go forward; do not slacken the pace for me unless I tell you." My challenge to you is that you move forward, and as it was with the Shunammite woman, the ride may be a bit bumpy but endure until you reach your destination.

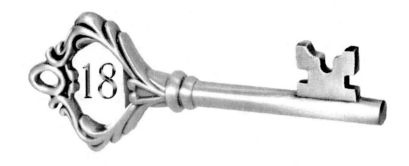

Don't Be Afraid
to Cross Cultural Boundaries

There is neither Jew nor Greek, there is neither slave nor free, there is neither male nor female; for you are all one in Christ Jesus.
Galatians 3:28

In John 4 the Samaritan Woman whom Jesus met at the well teaches us yet another important key to victorious living. When Jesus met her at the well He asked her for a drink of water. Her response was focused not on the water but on the fact that Jesus was a Jew and she a Samaritan. There was ethnic animosity and tensions between the two groups and they did not interact with one another. The Samaritan woman did not know Jesus personally; she only knew that He was a Jew and based her response to Him only on that fact.

Isn't it amazing that we as human beings can allow historical and ancestral tensions hinder us from relating to one another? Jesus' response to her was, "If you knew the gift of God, and who it is who says to you, 'Give Me a drink,' you would have asked him, and He would have given you living water" (John 4:10). To put it simply, "If you only knew "me"—not my ethnicity or where I'm from—"me." If you only knew who it is who stands before you and what I could do for you, you would be asking water of me" (paraphrased). The Samaritan woman could have missed out on a man who would forever change her life and the lives of others through her. Can you imagine the countless blessings we have missed out on only because we allowed cultural and historical differences to hinder us from getting to know other people?

We as daughters of God must not allow personal prejudices and unbiblical opinions of others to hinder us from building relationships. We might disagree with others' opinions but we can respectfully disagree and still choose to love. In our society differing religious views are one of the biggest boundaries that separate people. God has given each of us all free will to choose whom we will serve; yet as Christians, He has directed us to love everyone—Christian or not.

I have befriended both Christians and non-Christians. I have eaten with them, laughed with them, talked with them and determined that we all have the same basic needs. I cannot as a Christian separate myself from nonbelievers. In Mark 2:16 the Pharisees said of Jesus, "How is it that He eats and drinks with tax collectors and sinners?" As sinless as Jesus was He was not offended to sit among sinners because He was confident in who He was and thereby not threatened by others. When we as daughters of God are confident in who we are and have respect for others we will not be so easily threatened. We will be able to receive and love them as Christ demonstrated.

In Matthew 13:25-30 we are told of the parable of the sower who planted wheat in his fields only to have the enemy come and plant tares among the wheat. When the servants asked the master if they should pluck out the tares, the master responded, "Nay; lest while ye gather up the tares, ye root up also the wheat with them. Let both grow together until the harvest: and in the time of harvest I will say to the reapers, Gather ye together first the tares, and bind them in bundles to burn them: but gather the wheat into my barn." God is the one who will do the separating of believers from non-believers on the Day of Judgment; it is not for us to do.

As I look back upon my life, I can honestly say that had I had limited myself to interacting and befriending only Christians I would have missed out on great opportunities and blessings from those who may not have known God but had skills, abilities and knowledge that I needed to further my life and ministry. Had I limited myself to only those who were in the same financial class as I, I would have missed out on wisdom and knowledge from others who helped me get to my next level in life. Had I only communicated with people in my age group, I would have missed out on the wisdom and knowledge from those more mature who would help me throughout life and guide in my decision-making. Had I only dealt with individuals of my nationality and race, I would have missed out on the understanding of other cultural views. I am thankful I was willing to cross boundaries in these areas.

While evangelizing I have witnessed many Christians hesitate when it comes to witnessing to people outside of their social or economic class. It is easy for them to witness to a person they perceive as being from a lower or equal class, but they become intimidated when it comes to reaching someone they perceive as being from a higher class or further along the corporate ladder. Regardless of a person's social or economic class, we all have hurts and joys; we all need the same Jesus for salvation.

The people who God allows to cross our path are always there for a reason. It may not always be what they can do for us but sometimes what we can do for them. Jesus introduces the woman at the well to the God, who would quench her spiritual thirsting forever. Therefore, daughters of

God, I urge you to open your hearts and minds to know and relate to people from all walks of life; after all, there is only one Kingdom of God and it will be filled with many people having at least one thing in common: our belief in Jesus Christ as our Savior.

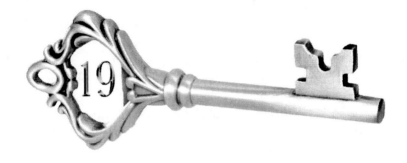

Be a Peacemaker

Blessed are the peacemakers, for they shall be called sons of God.
Matthew 5:9

In 1 Samuel 25, we learn of Abigail. Abigail was the beautiful, wise and intelligent wife of Nabal, a wealthy, ill-tempered businessman who owned 3,000 sheep and 1,000 goats. David and his army protected Nabal's flock and shepherds from the Philistine raiders while they were in Carmel. When David heard that Nabal was shearing his sheep, he sent 10 of his young men to inform Nabal of the protection that they had provided for his flock and shepherds and request a share in his food. Considering all that David and his army had done for Nabal, he had every right to expect to be received with gratitude and generosity. Instead Nabal insulted them and refused their request. Needless to say, David becomes furious at Nabal's response and purposed to kill Nabal and all of the men in his camp.

One of Nabal's servants informed Abigail of the goodness and protection David and his men had shown towards them while in Carmel, Nabal's response to David's request, and David's plan to destroy Nabal and all the men of the camp. Abigail, being the wise woman she was, acted quickly to right the wrong and directed her servants to gather the food and wine that Nabal should have given David and set out to personally deliver it with her apologies. As Abigail bowed before David, she bore the responsibility for Nabal's response to his request, apologized and pled for the life of the men of her camp. With wisdom, she spoke respectfully to David, so as to calm his anger. Abigail then took the blame upon herself for her husband's ungrateful response and accounted it to his natural weakness and lack of understanding. Abigail responded just as Jesus and Stephen the martyr did to those who took their lives: "Forgive him, for he knows not what he does." She commended David for his services, and prayed the blessings of God upon his life. Because of Abigail's actions, David received the offering and pardons the wrong done by Nabal. Abigail put her life on the line to settle Nabal's offence towards David thus demonstrating our next key to victory for women of God: to be a peacemaker.

Satan's plan is to bring discord and contentions in every place he can: on our jobs, in our homes, families, in marriages... even within the fellowship of believers. As the daughters of God we should always purpose to foster peace among others. There have been times in my life where I have had to intercede and apologize on behalf of others. On a recent occasion a family member had hurt someone's feelings with rude, insensitive remarks concerning their appearance. I knew that my family member was wrong in their actions but I also recognized that the family member did not intentionally set out to hurt this person's feelings.

I quickly apologized to the person for my family member's rude remarks and the person accepted the apology. As the daughters of God, we must do all that is within our power to foster peace among others and on behalf of others. God thinks highly of those who foster peace. In Matthew 5:9 Jesus says, "Blessed are the peacemakers for they shall be called the sons of God." What greater honor than being called a son or daughter of God?

Peacemakers calm the flames of anger. In Abigail's case, David not only pardoned Nabal's sin, he also thanked Abigail for interceding and stopping him from seeking vengeance on his own behalf and killing all the men in Nabal's camp—something he knew he would later regret. By interceding for the sake of peace you can keep others from doing a wrong that they would later regret.

Working in the prison system for many years, I have seen the after effects of those who acted in anger and did not seek a peaceable solution for handling disagreements and wrongdoings. I have listened to men and women, some of whom are serving a life sentence for acts committed out of fury that ended up costing them their future. I am sure that now they would have appreciated having someone intercede and speak wisdom to them then so they could have resolve their matters peaceably. Instead, they are serving years of their life locked behind bars due to the flames of their anger not being unkindled. I can only imagine where many of these young men and women would be if only a peacemaker had interceded.

Daughters of God, whether you witness wrongs in your personal or professional interactions, always speak up for the cause of peace. God will not forget your efforts towards peace and will surely bless you in your deeds. In Abigail's case, she was blessed not many days after her actions. Her husband died 10 days later, avenging David's cause, and David respected her enough to make her his wife. Daughters of God, when you take a stand for the sake of peace, your actions will not be forgotten. Just as God did for David, He will avenge wrongdoers. Do you remember a time in your life where you witnessed discord among others? What was your response? What will you do differently in the future?

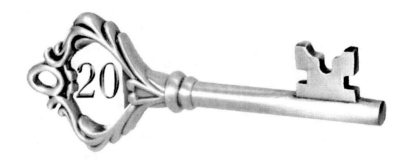

Determine to Leave the Past Behind

"Do not remember the former things, nor consider the things of old.
Isaiah 43:18

It can be said of a person walking in faith that there is nothing behind worth going back to because their future in God is always brighter. God is a progressive God and always has plans to take us to the next level not back to the old. Isaiah 43:18-19 says, "Do not remember the former things nor consider the things of old. Behold, I will do a new thing, now it shall spring forth; shall you not know it? I will even make a road in the wilderness and rivers in the desert."

If God's plan is to propel us into new places, why is it so hard for some of us to leave the old? I believe it is because Satan uses fear to cripple us: fear of the unknown, fear of change and fear that God does not have better planned for us. 2 Timothy 1:7 says, "For God has not given us the spirit of fear, but of love, and of power and of sound mind." Fear is the greatest opponent to our faith in Christ and the biggest hindrance to our moving forward towards the bright future God has planned for us.

Ruth was a great example of a woman who was determined to move forward and not to return to her past. After the death of her husband, her mother-in-law Naomi urged her to return to her people, her gods. Ruth's response was recorded in Ruth 1:16-17, "Entreat me not to leave you, or to turn back from following after you; for wherever you go, I will go; and wherever you lodge, I will lodge; Your people shall be my people, and your God, my God. Where you die, I will die, and there will I be buried. The Lord do so to me, and more also, if anything but death parts you and me."

Ruth had a strong determination to not return to her past and went with Naomi, her mother-in-law, to a land and a people that she was not familiar with thus demonstrating the next characteristic of a victorious woman: a determination to leave the past behind.

I deal with women daily who are stuck. They stay on jobs that limit their skills only because they've been there for many years and they've become complacent or are afraid to step out on faith. I have also seen women who step out but make backup plans just in case it doesn't work out. What I like about Ruth is that she had no plans to return to her past. She was ready and willing to move forward to a place that she had never thought of going. As Ruth moves to this unknown place God has a life-changing blessing awaiting her: a rich, new husband and a son.

Another woman within the Bible teaches us the danger of focusing on our past: Lot's wife. In Genesis 19 Lot and his family are directed by the angels of the Lord to leave Sodom, their hometown, to enter into the next city – and not to look back as they exit Sodom. As Lot and his family exit the city, Lot's wife disobeyed the directives of the Angel, looked back and instantly became a pillar of salt.

"Why salt?" I've wondered. Salt itself is a preserver or a substance that is used to keep items in an unchanged or unaltered state. Isn't it amazing that the very thing Lot's wife was turned into has the very effect on us when we continue to focus on our past and not move forward: we remain unchanged. When we, as daughters of God, continue to live in our past, whether mentally or physically, we are unable to evolve into the beautiful state that our Heavenly Father wants us to achieve.

When driving my automobile, I notice that regardless of where I want my wheels to go, they always seem to follow the direction in which I'm looking. If something catches my eye on the right, then my wheels go to my right. This very thing happens to us when we focus our attention and eyes on our past and what we left behind. We cannot move forward in God looking back. (Proverbs 4:25)

Regardless of the hurts and the pains of your past it is time to quit focusing your attention there and move forward. You will never reach your promised land if you are always looking back. What you have done in your past and what has been done to you matter not anymore. To move forward you must make the decision to forgive others, to forgive yourself and to receive God's forgiveness.

I have seen so many women who have given their lives to God yet refuse to allow Him to deliver them from their pasts. They sit and hear the Word of God week after week yet refuse to receive the truth for their lives and remain unchanged both mentally and spiritually. Ruth could have chosen to hold on to the hurt of losing her husband and become bitter; instead she moved forward to receive the blessings that God had awaiting her.

What life-changing event have you prolonged or missed out on because of your focus on the past? What opportunity has presented itself to you that you allowed your past to keep you from entering into? Some of us have refused to enter into new relationships, seek new jobs, travel to new places, start new businesses or try something new all because of fear and focusing on the past. Daughters of God, I challenge you to identify those areas in your life in which you have become complacent and continue to dwell in the past and take a leap of faith forward into the blessed places God has awaiting you.

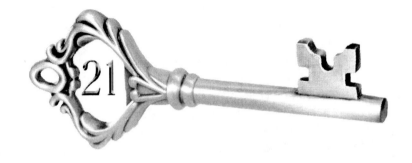

Have Confidence in God's Words

Forever, O Lord, Your word is settled in heaven. **Psalm 119:89**

In Judges 4 we are introduced to our next victorious women of the Bible: Deborah. We don't hear much of women in the Bible being involved in battles but Deborah and Jeal were the exceptions. They were instrumental in the Army of Israel's victory in the battle against Sisera and his troops. Deborah was a Prophetess and judge of Israel during a time when the children of Israel were being held captive by Jabin, the king of Canaan. The Prophetess, Deborah, informed Barak, the leader of Israel's army, that he has been commanded by God to deploy 10,000 troops at Mt. Tabor and fight against Sisera, the leader of Jabin's army. God, through the Prophetess Deborah told Barak that he would deliver Sisera into his hand. Although Barak heard the Word of God on the matter spoken by Deborah, he insisted that he would only go up to the battle if Deborah went with him. Deborah willingly accepted the invitation and delivered yet another message from God to Barak in Judges 4:9-10:

So she said, "I will surely go with you; nevertheless there will be no glory for you in the journey you are taking, for the Lord will sell Sisera into the hand of a woman." Then Deborah arose and went with Barak to Kedesh. And Barak called Zebulun and Naphtali to Kedesh; he went up with ten thousand men under his command, and Deborah went up with him.

Deborah's willingness to accompany Barak to battle was not because of her trust in her own abilities but because she was confident in the Word of God. Although Deborah was a woman she possessed the most powerful weapon in the universe, a word of victory from God. Hebrews 4:12 says, "For the Word of God is living and powerful, and sharper than any two-edged sword, piercing even to the division of soul and spirit, and of joints and marrow, and is a discerner of the thoughts and intents of the heart." As a Prophetess, Deborah was accustomed to hearing the voice of God and was confident of its truth and strength. Deborah understood that once the Word of God had been spoken on the matter it was settled, thus demonstrating our next key to victory: have confidence in God's Words.

When the time of battle had arrived, Deborah said to Barak, "Up! For this is the day in which the Lord has delivered Sisera into your hand.

Has not the Lord gone out before you?" (Judges 4:14). So Barak went down from Mount Tabor with 10,000 men following him. Deborah was a woman with total confidence in God's Word! Her confidence was contagious; the army of Israel, under Barak's direction, went when she said "Go!"

So Barak went down from Mount Tabor with ten thousand men following him. And the Lord routed Sisera and all his chariots and all his army with the edge of the sword before Barak; and Sisera alighted from his chariot and fled away on foot. But Barak pursued the chariots and the army as far as Harosheth Hagoyim, and all the army of Sisera fell by the edge of the sword; not a man was left. However, Sisera had fled away on foot to the tent of Jael, the wife of Heber the Kenite; for there was peace between Jabin king of Hazor and the house of Heber the Kenite. Judges 4:14-17

Many Christians say they believe in God yet have doubts when it comes to stepping out on His Word and directives for their life. John 1:1 says, "In the beginning was the Word, and the Word was with God, and the Word was God." God and His Word are one; we cannot separate the two. If we say that we truly believe in God then we also must believe His Word.

Satan's motive since the beginning of time has been to deceive women into believing that the Word of God is not true, he began with the first woman: Eve. He convinced Eve that the words spoken by God were not true. In Genesis 3:1 Satan asked Eve, "Has God indeed said, 'You shall not eat of every tree of the garden?'" Note that Satan began the deception by causing Eve to question the Word of God.

Any time we question the written or spoken Word of God concerning our life we open ourselves up to deception. Eve responds to Satan with, "We may eat the fruit of the trees of the garden; but of the fruit of the tree which is in the midst of the garden. God has said, 'You shall not eat it, nor shall you touch it, lest you die." Eve, like many of us, knew what God had said concerning the matter and had no problems following God's directives until she begin communicating with the enemy. Then the serpent said to her, "You will not surely die. For God knows that in the day you eat of it your eyes will be opened, and you will be like God, knowing good and evil." Satan blatantly presents to Eve that the word spoken by God were not true and that God was in some way holding back His best from her.

Eve then began evaluating the situation from her natural perspective and determined that God was withholding something good from her. 'So when the woman saw that the tree was good for food, that it was pleasant to the eyes, and a tree desirable to make one wise, she took of its fruit and ate. She also gave to her husband with her, and he ate" (Genesis 3:6). Eve ate the forbidden fruit and so came the fall of man from God's perfect will.

Whenever we base our decisions upon our natural perspective as opposed to all knowing God's Word and directives we will not experience God's best in our life. God's Word is filled with promises if we only obey and believe. We cannot afford to miss God's best during this season of our life.

As the leader of a singles ministry, I frequently hear singles that had previously believed God for a mate become discouraged in the process and begin to base God's ability on their natural circumstances.

"I'm getting older."

"There's a lack of Christian men in the church."

"Maybe God does not want me to marry."

Some of them then default on every promise God has given them in this area and pursue to find a mate of their own only to their demise. Daughters of God, know that our Heavenly Father desires for you to have His best, He's always got our best interests in mind and He promises us in Psalms 37:4 that if we delight ourselves in Him, He will give us the desires of our heart. Don't allow the enemy to deceive you into settling for less in any areas of your life where God has promised blessings, whether spoken to you personally or through His Word. The Word of God is for you and according to Matthew 24:35, "Heaven and earth will pass away, but My words will by no means pass away." God's promises have no expiration date—as long as you believe God's Word, you too can walk confidently and receive His promises.

To be victorious in life, we as daughters of God must receive the Word of God as the first and final authority in all of our decisions. What words has God spoken over your life? What has He directed you to do? What was your response?

When you believe God and stand confidently on every word He has spoken to you, you too will move forward towards your victory. Some of you may wonder, "How can I increase my confidence in God's Word?" You increase your confidence in God's Word by hearing the Word consistently and cultivating a relationship with God through fellowship and prayer.

In Romans 10:17 it says, "So then faith comes by hearing, and hearing by the Word of God." Hearing the Word of God must become a routine in your life to believe and become victorious. The more time we spend in the presence of God and in hearing His Word the greater our faith and confidence in Him will become. The Word of God contains the answers to every situation and issue we face. When we truly believe and have confidence in God's Word, we will be like Deborah and step out confidently on God's Word.

God has Equipped You with Everything You Need for Victory

Have I not commanded you? "Be strong and of good courage; do not be afraid, nor be dismayed, for the Lord your God is with you wherever you go." Joshua 1:9

In Judges 4, after Barak refused to go to battle without Deborah, Deborah informed Barak that God would allow Sisera be sold into the hands of a woman. That woman was none other than Jael, the wife of Heber - a Kenite.

> *However, Sisera had fled away on foot to the tent of Jael, the wife of Heber the Kenite; for there was peace between Jabin king of Hazor and the house of Heber the Kenite. 18 And Jael went out to meet Sisera, and said to him, "Turn aside, my lord, turn aside to me; do not fear." And when he had turned aside with her into the tent, she covered him with a blanket. 19 Then he said to her, "Please give me a little water to drink, for I am thirsty." So she opened a jug of milk, gave him a drink, and covered him. 20 And he said to her, "Stand at the door of the tent, and if any man comes and inquires of you, and says, 'Is there any man here?' you shall say, 'No.' 21 Then Jael, Heber's wife, took a tent peg and took a hammer in her hand, and went softly to him and drove the peg into his temple, and it went down into the ground; for he was fast asleep and weary. So he died. 22 And then, as Barak pursued Sisera, Jael came out to meet him, and said to him, "Come, I will show you the man whom you seek." And when he went into her tent, there lay Sisera, dead with the peg in his temple.* Judges 4:17-18 -22

Jael finalized the victory for Israel in their battle against Sisera by killing their leader Sisera thus demonstrating our next key to victory: God has equipped us with everything we need to be victorious.

I am sure that Jael had no clue the battle she would have to face on the day of her encounter with Sisera; nevertheless, she was ready. Many times in our lives we have to face unplanned battles and encounters and if we allow ourselves to be overshadowed by the status or strength of our opponent we will give up before the fight. Jael could have focused on the military experience of Sisera along with the fact that he was a man and not even attempt the fight. Instead she used the skills and intelligence God had already instilled within her to gain her victory.

If we as Women choose to focus on the strengths of our enemies or the magnitude of our battles, we devalue the strength and power of our Heavenly Father. Philippians 4:13 says, "I can do all things through

Christ who strengthens me." Women of God, claim this as your truth. Our Heavenly Father will not put more upon us than we are able to bear—when it feels like He has, we need to look to Him for strength. Although Jael was a woman, God knew that she could gain the victory over Sisera because He had already prepared her with the weapons required.

⚷ She had her womanly charm to win his trust and lure him

into her camp.

⚷ She used the knowledge she possessed about the effects

of heavy milk to make him sleepy.

⚷ She covered him so that he would not see her coming.

⚷ She used her strength and experience with using a peg

and hammer to pound a peg through his temple.

Women of God, what strength dwells within you? What skills, abilities and knowledge has the Heavenly Father equipped you with? I guarantee that if you take an inventory of your strengths and abilities, you will see that you have everything you need to conquer your battles.

Maintain a calm peace like Jeal did and believe that you can do it…that you can have the victory. Know that it is not the size of your battle that matters but the Word of your Heavenly Father. The Word of God had already been released through Deborah that "Sisera shall be sold into the hands of a Woman." Through her own abilities Jael could not have subdued Sisera; it was the power of God's Word that brought the victory. Jael was only the vessel through which God accomplished this feat.

What words has the Father spoken over your life? Know that if God spoke it He is well able to do it. Our Heavenly Father's Word is the most powerful force on the face of the earth; as He has spoken, so shall it be. We as women of God have to hold on to the promises of God and trust His Word above our strengths and abilities.

Many times I have received prophetic words from God of these great plans that He has for my life; the great exploits that I will do through Him, the places I am to travel, the lives I am to touch. In response to several, I have wondered, "How?" I know that on my own my future is doom and gloom, but with my Heavenly Father "I can do all things through Christ." God has equipped and is equipping me with everything I need to be victorious in every battle that comes my way. Women of God regardless of the battles or challenges you are facing, keep moving forward. Know that if God has brought a battle your way He has also equipped you with the weapons needed to gain the victory.

Sisera made the biggest mistake of his life when he underestimated the power of a woman. Although Jael acted like an innocent woman, she demonstrated her strength by killing Sisera with one blow of a peg through his temple. In doing so, she fulfilled the prophecy of Deborah that God would sell Sisera to a woman.

Can you remember a time in your life that you have had to face a situation or challenge that overwhelmed you? As you look back over that situation—whether you faced the challenge or threw in the towel—do you now feel that God had prepared you with the weapons to be victorious in that situation? What battles or challenges are you facing at this moment? What skills, knowledge and abilities will you draw from within to fight it? Women of God, I challenge you to consider all that God has placed within you and face those battles. If God brought it to you, He will make you victorious if you trust in him.

Timing Is Everything

He who keeps his command will experience nothing harmful; and a wise man's heart discerns both time and judgment, because for every matter there is a time and judgment, though the misery of man increases greatly.
Ecclesiastes 8:5-6

The next key to victory demonstrated by Jael was the understanding that timing is everything. Although Jael quickly devised a plan to destroy Sisera, she had to wait until the right time to kill him. Had she attempted to attack Sisera with the hammer and tent peg prematurely, he could have over powered her and taken her life. She thoroughly assessed the situation before her, assessed Sisera's weaknesses, and went to work.

Jael first used her femininity to win Sisera's trust. She invited him into her tent, provided a place for him to rest and covered him with a mantle. After he asked her for a drink of water, she brought him heavy milk instead. Ladies, we all know what milk does for babies—it makes them sleepy. Sisera was no exception. After drinking the milk he fell asleep, putting himself in a vulnerable position whereby he would not even see an attack coming. As Sisera was sleeping, Jael drove a tent peg through his temple with a hammer. He never knew what hit him.

We often have goals we want to accomplish in our lives but we get too eager and make premature moves that cost us our victory. Had Jael attempted to attack Sisera prior to him falling asleep, he may have destroyed her. I am sure that the brief span of time that lapsed prior to Sisera falling asleep seemed like eternity to Jael; but she waited patiently.

As daughters of God we must understand that with God there is a time for everything. God has a plan for each of our lives. That plan requires our cooperation and trust in His timing to gain total victory. We have all had things in our lives that we desired to accomplish, whether it is career growth, marriage, family or a ministerial opportunity. Remember that timing is everything.

Ecclesiastes 3:1 says, "To everything there is a season, a time for every purpose under heaven." Daughters of God, I urge you to wait for God's perfect timing in all that you desire to accomplish. Although you may get anxious at times, remember that the Father will not withhold from you any good thing (Psalm 84:11). Our enemy, Satan, desires us to be anxious and step out prematurely.

Philippians 4:6-7 says that we are to, "Be anxious for nothing, but in everything by prayer and supplication, with thanksgiving, let your requests be made known to God; and the peace of God, which surpasses all understanding, will guard your hearts and minds through Christ Jesus." Having been a woman who made many decisions out of anxiousness, I can truly say that doing things in God's timing is much better. I have witnessed individuals who left their jobs prematurely and suffered financially, rushed into marriage and married the wrong person, and who made large purchases too early only to soon after realize that they couldn't afford it. Ecclesiastes 3:11 says of God, "He makes all things beautiful in its time." Let me encourage you to wait on God's timing in whatever decisions you are facing, His timing is always perfect. Do you recall a time when you stepped out too early? What was the outcome? What would you now do differently?

Be Persistent

Then He spoke a parable to them, that men always ought to pray and not lose heart, saying: "There was in a certain city a judge who did not fear God nor regard man. Now there was a widow in that city; and she came to him, saying, 'Get justice for me from my adversary.' And he would not for a while; but afterward he said within himself, 'Though I do not fear God nor regard man, yet because this widow troubles me I will avenge her, lest by her continual coming she weary me.'" Then the Lord said, "Hear what the unjust judge said. And shall God not avenge His own elect who cry out day and night to Him, though He bears long with them? I tell you that He will avenge them speedily. Nevertheless, when the Son of Man comes, will He really find faith on the earth?" Luke 18:1-8

In Mark 7, Jesus was resting when a Greek woman approached him, fell at His feet and asked that He cast a devil out of her daughter. Jesus' response to the woman is recorded in Mark 7:27, "Let the children be filled first, for it is not good to take the children's bread and throw it to the little dogs." Jesus actually compared the Greek woman to a dog but note that she did not get intimidated nor did it stop her from her pursuit of requesting deliverance for her daughter. She responded to Jesus with, "Yes, Lord, yet even the little dogs under the table eat from the children's crumbs" (Mark 7:28). This woman had a need and knew that Jesus was able to meet her need; therefore she didn't get offended or intimidated by Jesus' response. She persevered until Jesus delivered her daughter from the devil. If the woman had accepted Jesus' initial denial she would have missed out on her daughter's deliverance. She demonstrated our next key to victory: be persistent.

Daughters of God, how many times have you allowed a negative response from others to deter you from your desires, your dreams and your passions? We pursue after something and the person holding the keys to our desires or those from whom we sought encouragement use intimidating words, causing us to feel as though the desire is not for us. We then begin taking the negative comments personally or become too intimidated to pursue further or argue our case. I like this Greek woman because she wanted deliverance for her daughter so badly that it did not matter that Jesus likened her to a dog. She didn't take it personally but responded with, "Yes, Lord, yet even the little dogs under the table eat from the children's crumbs" (Mark 7:28). Jesus then told her in Mark 7:29-30, "For this saying go your way; the demon has gone out of your daughter." We learn that she then sees her daughter lying on the bed free of all demons.

I have seen dreams shattered because someone didn't get the initial response they wanted. My late grandmother told me the story of how she obtained a job at a prominent worksite in her younger years. She would go by the ship yard every day to inquire if they had a job opening, to which she was daily given the same answer: "No." She continued to pursue her efforts in getting the job until one day, after seeing her persistence and knowing that she was not going to give up, the boss hired her. If she had accepted that the prior rejections meant the job was not for her, she would have missed out on the opportunity to get the job she had long desired. I have shared my career dreams with some people only to have them respond negatively or reflect that I was not good enough because they did not feel that I could do it. Although the negative comments may have hurt they did not stop me from pursuing my dreams. Daughters of God don't give up on your desires and dreams because you didn't get the encouragement or the response you wanted from others. Do as the Greek woman did: plead your case, be persistent and don't accept "No" for an answer.

Listen to the Wisdom of Your Elders

The law of the wise is a fountain of life, to turn one away from the snares of death. **Proverbs 13:14**

On the bulletin board at my office someone had written a question to business owners asking, "If you could go back to when you were 18 and graduating high school, what would you have done differently?" One of the answers was, "I would have listened more closely to my elders." I am sure that many of you can relate to this response.

I remember as a teenager when our parents or another mature adult would try and instill wisdom within us we thought that they just didn't understand. We failed to realize the fact that they had already walked through the stage of life that we were currently traveling. In Ecclesiastes 1:9 the preacher says, "That which has been is what will be, that which is done is what will be done, and there is nothing new under the sun." The older I get the more I understand that we face the same issues just different times.

Imagine what life would be like if you knew the godly and wise way to handle every situation that comes your way. Well guess what? You can have the answers of how to best handle life situations and it comes through your ability to listen and apply the wisdom of your elders. There is someone who has been through every situation that you are currently facing and can give you godly wisdom on what they have seen work in their lives or observed in others' lives.

Every woman should have a mentor. Merriam-Webster (2015) defines a mentor as "someone who teaches or gives help and advice to a less experienced and often younger person." Two of the women in our study had notable mentors who gave them the wisdom they needed to acquire their victories: Esther and Ruth.

You should remember from our earlier lessons, Esther had Mordecai and Ruth had Naomi. In our study of Esther we noted that Mordecai had given Esther the directive to not reveal her family or her people and advised her regarding how she could save the lives of the Jews. Naomi gave Ruth the womanly advice she needed to get her future husband Boaz's attention. Esther and Ruth both could have ignored Mordecai's and Naomi's directives, but both knew their elders loved them and had their best interests in mind.

As daughters of God we need to open our hearts and minds to learn from those with experiences in life. We each should have a person in our life whom we can go to for directions and advice. I have gained from the advice of many people, both younger and older, with wisdom to share. Wisdom is not always attained from the mature in age but those mature in handling life's experiences.

I remember an older man who lived next-door to us growing up whom I thoroughly enjoyed listening to – such wisdom came from his mouth. He was not a millionaire but he had acquired vast wisdom during his 80+ years of life. The bit I learned from him still resonates in my ears today.

I have heard older people say, "You can listen and learn from the mistakes of others or you can learn the hard way." This means you can either let others do the learning and teach you, or you can learn the lesson after you make the mistake and pay the consequences. I have always been the type person who preferred to listen and learn from others. I encourage you to do so as well.

As a mentor, I am open to sharing with others the wisdom and knowledge that God has bestowed upon me, although one thing that I hate is wasting my time by sharing wisdom with those who do not appreciate it. In Matthew 7:6 Jesus refers to this as "casting your pearls before swine." These are the women with whom others share their wisdom and knowledge but they are unappreciative of it. They prefer to do things their way, which time after time proves to be wrong.

I have a young friend, Sue, who would come to me consistently to share her problems and then ask me what she should do. I would impart wisdom on the best way I have found to handle the matters only for Sue to do things her way and later regret that she did not listen. Proverbs 28:26 says, "He who trusts in his own heart is a fool, but whoever walks wisely will be delivered." Sue's way always got her deeper into trouble. I finally had to ask Sue why she continued coming to me and wasting my time when she was going to do things her way anyway. She acknowledged that this was a problem for her and that if she had applied my imparted wisdom to the situations, she would have been further along in her life.

Ladies, when you seek the wisdom of others please be good soil into which others are willing to plant wisdom. As you begin to listen and learn from those with life experiences, you will learn lessons that will save you heartache and wasted time. Proverbs 13:14 says, "The law of the wise is a fountain of life, to turn one away from the snares of death." Daughters of God, I encourage you to humble yourself and identify a person or two who have the wisdom of God and can assist you in reaching your next level.

Cultivate a Heart of Gratitude

Make a joyful shout to the Lord, all you lands! Serve the Lord with gladness; come before His presence with singing. Know that the Lord, He is God; it is He who has made us, and not we ourselves, we are His people and the sheep of His pasture. Enter into His gates with thanksgiving, and into His courts with praise. Be thankful to Him, and bless His name. For the Lord is good; His mercy is everlasting, and His truth endures to all generations. **Psalm 100**

As daughters of God we should always have a heart of gratitude towards our Heavenly Father and others. 1 Thessalonians 5:18 says that we should "give thanks in everything, for this is the will of God in Christ Jesus for you." Although things may not always go our way, we must remember that because we are the daughters of God, all things are working together for our good. In our daily communions with our Heavenly Father we should always give thanks and show appreciation for what God is doing and has done on our behalf. Hebrews 13:15 declares, "Therefore by Him let us continually offer the sacrifice of praise to God, that is, the fruit of our lips, giving thanks to His name."

It is easy for us to go before God with a long list of the things we want Him to do for us and never consider or give thanks for what He has already done. Throughout our study we saw thanksgiving expressed in various ways: Mary the Mother of Jesus and the Prophetess Deborah expressed their gratitude to God in songs while Sarai, Abraham's wife, could only laugh. In whatever way the spirit leads you, express thankfulness to God.

Coming before God with gratitude and thanksgiving sets the environment whereby the hands of God are opened towards you. I have noticed that when dealing with people on an everyday basis, being thankful and appreciating what others do on your behalf—regardless of how small—gives them a desire to want to do and give more.

I had the pleasure of spending a morning with my two nieces during which the eldest, Tsatsi, was cooking her favorite dish. Her younger sister asked for some and although Tsatsi had another entire package of this dish she told Kourtni that she could have only half of one. As Tsatsi returned to the kitchen to cook, Kourtni began talking to us about what a great cook Tsatsi was. She went on and on about how Tsatsi makes the best eggs she has ever tasted. She reviewed with us the steps that her sister takes in making these great eggs. Although Tsatsi was in the next room, she could hear every word Kourtni said concerning how great her eggs were. Minutes later Tsatsi came in and gave Kourtni the entire package of her favorite dish. Kourtni smiled and replied, "Thank you."

This very thing happens when we have a heart of appreciation and thanksgiving towards God and others: it forces their hands to open and release more blessings. When you go before God daily in prayer, I challenge you to begin your prayers with thanksgiving, recognizing the blessings that God has bestowed upon you. Even when I am in a crisis situation in my life and have much on my mind, going before God with a list of things to give Him thanks and honor for changes the entire atmosphere and increases my faith in the abilities of God and in the great love that He has towards me. Having a heart of gratitude makes it easy to offer praise and worship before God because a heart of gratitude recognizes him as God. Thanksgiving also increases our faith as we consider the things God has already done on our behalf. It reminds us of God's power, strength and loving heart towards us His daughters. Daughters of God always find a reason to offer thanksgiving to God.

Go Forth and Be Victorious

We have learned a lot throughout these chapters. My prayer is that you will not only read these keys but act upon them. As you begin applying these biblical keys to your everyday life God will open doors for you that you never thought would open and you too can declare the song of Mary.

My soul magnifies the Lord, and my spirit has rejoiced in God my Savior. For He has regarded the lowly state of His maidservant; for behold, henceforth all generations will call me blessed. For He who is mighty has done great things for me, and holy is His name. And His mercy is on those who fear Him from generation to generation. He has shown strength with His arm; He has scattered the proud in the imagination of their hearts. He has put down the mighty from their thrones, and exalted the lowly. He has filled the hungry with good things, and the rich He has sent away empty. He has helped His servant Israel, in remembrance of His mercy, as He spoke to our fathers, to Abraham and to his seed forever. Luke 1:46-55

About the Author

BRENDA K. FIELDS

Brenda Fields has been gifted by God to serve in many roles within the body of Christ. She is an Author, Teacher, Administrator, Organizer and Mentor.

As a Five Fold Ministry Teacher, Brenda has a passion to see the Word of God taught with accuracy and simplicity so it can be understood and applied to the lives of Spirit-filled believers. Her teachings challenge believers to go to the next level in their faith by believing and stepping into the promises of God. She has taught on such topics as Understanding Spiritual Gifts, Understanding Dreams and Visions, Using your Spiritual Gifts as Evangelistic Tools and Increasing Your Faith.

Outside of the church, Ms. Fields has served as a Manager of Performance / Quality Improvement for more than 12 years. She combines her experience in organizational development and performance improvement to assist churches in developing structure and restoring order so they can achieve their God-given missions. Her goal is to see the church function as a healthy body, fitly joined together and growing.

Ms. Fields currently resides in Montgomery Alabama where she is the Founder and Owner of Dream Connectors Realty, LLC. She is a graduate of Wallace College in Selma Alabama and Alabama State University, where she earned an Associate's in Nursing and a Bachelor's in Health Information Management, respectively.

I can do all things through Christ who strengthens me. Philippians 4:13

For information on booking or to contact the Author:
Email: AuthorBrendaFields@gmail.com **Fax:** 1-866-823-5529
Facebook: Author Brenda Fields

References

The following version of The Holy Bible was used within the pages of this book. New King James Version (NKJV)

The Free Dictionary (2003 – 2015). http://www.thefreedictionary.com/servant

Mirriam-Webster (2015). http://www.merriam-webster.com/dictionary

Workbook

Keys to Becoming
a Victorious Woman

Self-Development Guide
Moving Forth into Victory

Keys to Becoming a Victorious Woman

Lessons Learned from Women of the Bible

Self-Development Guide

This self-development guide is designed to assist you in implementing the 26 keys discussed in this book to your life and be transformed into the victorious women God created you to be.

You are encouraged to read the book in its entirety prior to proceeding to the self-development section. After completing the book; then review each section along with the self- development guide to assist you in the development of each key in your life.

To assist you through your self-development process, this guide is presented as follows:

- **Scriptures** to study and further enhance your knowledge of what God's Word says concerning each key presented

- **Discussion Questions** to assess what you have learned from each lesson

- **Self-Analysis Questions** which allow you to evaluate yourself and identify those areas where self-development is needed

- **Daily Journal** to identify how you will begin implementing each of the 26 keys in your life and to monitor your progress in each area.

You are encouraged to answer each of the self-analysis questions honestly and deal with personal issues as God reveals them to you.

This guide can be used individually or discussed in a group setting in which participants share life experiences and grow from one another. If you are conducting a group study of this book, I encourage you to gather with your group after reading each section and discuss what each of you has learned, share any relevant life experiences and discuss how you will each begin implementing the keys in your life. This study can be presented over a 26-week period or in a weekend workshop setting based upon the needs of your group.

Keys to Becoming
a Victorious Woman
Lessons Learned from Women of the Bible
Self-Development Guide

Lesson 1 - Total Submission to God's Plan for Your Life

Lesson 2 - Daily Communion with God

Lesson 3 - Seek God's Favor

Lesson 4 - Know Your Purpose

Lesson 5 - Recognize the Greater Cause: "It's Not About You"

Lesson 6 - Stay Focused on Your Goals

Lesson 7 - Be Faithful Over Your Responsibilities

Lesson 8 - Develop a Servant's Heart

Lesson 9 - Go Above and Beyond Expectations

Lesson 10 - Be Hospitable Toward Others

Lesson 11 - When Opportunity Knocks, Don't Delay

Lesson 12 - Be a Woman of Your Word

Lesson 1

Total Submission to God's Plan for Your Life

What do the following scriptures teach us in regard to totally submitting our life to God?

Luke Chapter 1

Galatians 2:19-20

Proverbs 19-21

Romans 12:1-2 114

Matthew 6:33

Romans 6:13

2 Corinthians 5:14-15

Matthew 10:38-39

Mark 14:36

Discussion Questions

1. How would you define total submission to God?

2. What made Mary willing to totally surrender to God's plan for her life?

3. What are some reasons that people fail to totally surrender their life to God?

4. What did Mary lose by totally surrendering her life to God?

5. What did Mary gain by totally surrendering her life to God?

Self-Analysis

1. Has there ever been a time in your life when you had things all planned out only to have God interject His plan? If so, how did you respond? What was the outcome?

2. Are there any areas of your life that you have not totally surrendered to God?

3. What are you experiencing in those areas?

4. What is currently hindering you from totally surrendering your all to God?

5. How would your life change if you totally surrendered to God's plan for every area of your life?

Daily Journal

Lesson 2

Daily Communion with God

What do the following scriptures teach us in regard to communion with God?

Revelation 3:20

Matthew 11:28-30

Psalm 8:4

Psalm 145:18

Hebrews 11:6

Isaiah 55:6

James 4:8

Discussion Questions

1. What is the purpose of prayer and communion with God?

2. How does God respond to us coming before His presence for the purpose of communion?

3. What are some common excuses people use as to why they do not spend quality time with God?

Self-Analysis

1. How much time do you currently spend in prayer with God on a daily basis?

2. How has your current level of fellowship and communion with God impacted your life and the lives of those around you?

3. How would your life and the lives of those around you be impacted if you increased your time of fellowship and communion with God?

4. What has hindered you from spending quality time in the presence of God?

5. How would you feel if God removed everything that is currently hindering your ability to commune and fellowship with Him from your life? Could you live without it?

6. What is your response to God when He calls you to pray at times that you may not be convenient for you?

7. Do you feel that this is an acceptable response to God?

8. What changes are you willing to make in your life to increase your time of communion and fellowship with your Heavenly Father?

Daily Journal

Lesson 3

Seek God's Favor

What do the following scriptures teach us in regard to acquiring Gods favor upon our life?

Esther 1-10

Proverbs 8:35

Psalm 89:16-17

Proverbs 11:27

Joshua 1:8

Proverbs 12:2

Proverbs 3:3-4

Psalms 5:11-12

Psalms 37:4

Psalm 44:1-3

Discussion Questions

1. What does it mean to have the favor of God upon your life?

2. How does the favor of God differ from the love of God?

3. How was the favor of God shown in the life of Esther?

4. How does a person acquire the favor of God?

Self-Analysis

1. Discuss a time in your life when you experienced God's favor?

2. In which areas of your life do you currently need the favor of God?

3. As a Daughter of God, what actions are you willing to take to acquire the favor of God upon your life?

Daily Journal

Lesson 4

Know Your Purpose

What do the following scriptures teach us in regard to God's purpose for our life?

Esther 4-5

Proverbs 19:21

Jeremiah 1:5

Jeremiah 29:11

Romans 8:28

Ephesians 1:11

John 6:38

Acts 26: 12-18

John 15:16

Isaiah 43:17

Psalm 139:13-16

Philippians 1:6

Proverbs 16:9

Ephesians 2:20

Discussion Questions

1. How did Esther's attitude towards entering the King inner courts change after Mordecai presents to her that maybe she was chosen to be in the Kingdom for such a time as this?

2. How did Esther prepare to fulfill this purpose?

3. What was the outcome of Esther putting her life on the line to fulfill her purpose?

4. How can a person discover their purpose?

5. What are some of the consequences of not fulfilling your God ordained purpose?

Self-Analysis

1. Have you inquired of God concerning His plan and purpose for you during this season of your life? If so, what is your purpose? If not, why?

2. How are you preparing yourself to fulfill your God ordained purpose or calling?

3. Are you willing to put your life on the line as Esther did to fulfill your purpose? Why or why not?

Daily Journal

Lesson 5

Recognize the Greater Cause "It's Not About You"

What do the following scriptures teach us in regard to our responsibility when leading others?

Esther 1-10

Mark 10:42-45

Matthew 20:20-28

Mark 9:35

Philippians 2:3-11

John 13:12-17

Luke 12:48

Discussion Questions

1. What was Esther's response when she realized that God had placed her in the kingdom for a greater cause?

2. How did Esther's being in the kingdom impact the lives of others?

3. What was Esther's attitude toward putting her life on the line for the Jews?

Self-Analysis

1. In what position(s) has God currently placed you?

2. Prior to reading this book, why did you feel that God chose you for this position?

3. As you assess your current position or role, why do you now feel that God chose you for this position?

4. If others were questioned as to what impact you have had in their life, what would they say?

5. Have you ever had to speak up for the cause of another? If so, how did the person whom you spoke up for respond?

6. Do you remember a time in your life where you should have spoken up for another person but refused? What was the outcome? What would you do differently today?

Daily Journal

Lesson 6

Stay Focused on Your Goals

What do the following scriptures teach us in regard to focusing on our goals?

Esther 5

Proverbs 4:25-27

Proverbs 3:1-6

Proverbs 16:3

Hebrews 12:1-2

Matthew 6:33

Philippians 4:13

Discussion Questions

1. What was Esther's goal when she went before the King?

2. What diversions were presented to Esther as she entered the King's court? How did Esther respond?

3. Why was it important that Esther stay focused on her goal when making her request of the King?

4. What are some common diversions that cause people to lose sight of their goals?

Self-Analysis

1. What are three of your current goals?

2. What actions have you taken to accomplish these goals?

3. What diversions has the enemy sent your way to divert your attention from fulfilling your goals? How have you responded to these diversions?

4. What was the impact of your response to these diversions on the accomplishment of your goals?

5. How will you respond to diversions in the future?

Daily Journal

Lesson 7

Be Faithful Over Your Responsibilities

What do the following scriptures teach us in regard to the importance of being faithful over our responsibilities?

Genesis 24:11-15

Proverbs 22:29

1 Corinthians 4:1-2

Matthew 25:14-30

Luke 12:41-48

Luke 16:1-13

Colossians 3:23-25

Colossians 3:17

Discussion Questions

1. What was Rebecca's attitude towards fulfilling her responsibilities?

2. How did Rebecca's faithfulness to the small things prepare her for her future responsibilities?

3. Identify factors that cause some people to become slothful in fulfilling their responsibilities?

4. What are the consequences of being slothful to fulfill our responsibilities?

Self-Analysis

1. What responsibilities are you currently assigned?

2. On a scale of 1-10 with 10 being highest, how would you rate your level of faithfulness in fulfilling your current responsibilities?

3. In any areas where you rated yourself less than 10, what steps are you willing to take to increase you faithfulness?

4. Have you ever missed out on a great opportunity due to being slothful? If yes, discuss?

Daily Journal

Lesson 8

Develop A Servant's Heart

What do the following scriptures teach us in regard to serving others?

Genesis 24

1 Peter 5:6

Philippians 2:5-11

Luke 10:30-37

Galatians 5:13-14

1 Peter 4:10

Mark 10:43-45

Mark 9:35

John 13:12-17

Luke 22:27

Discussion Questions

1. What does it mean to serve others?

2. In what ways did Rebecca demonstrate the heart of a servant towards Abraham's servant?

3. What did you learn from this lesson about Rebecca's heart toward serving?

4. Why do many people find it hard to serve others?

5. In what ways did Jesus demonstrate being a servant to others?

Self-Analysis

1. On a scale of 1-10 with 10 being the highest, how would you rate your hearts' attitude toward serving others?

2. In what way has your view towards serving changed since this study?

3. What current opportunities do you have to serve others?

Daily Journal

Lesson 9

Go above and Beyond Expectations

What do the following scriptures teach us in regard to going above and beyond expectations?

Genesis 24

Daniel 6:3-4

Colossians 3:17, 23-34

Ecclesiastes 9:10

1 Corinthians 10:31

1 Corinthians 15:58

Discussion Questions

1. In what ways did Rebecca exceed the expectation of Abraham's servant?

2. What does a willingness to exceed expectations say about a person's heart towards the service they are providing?

3. Why do some people only do enough to meet the minimum requirement of their duty? What does this say of that person's heart towards the service they are providing?

Self-Analysis

1. Has anyone ever exceeded your expectation in performance of a service? What was your response?

2. What is your current attitude towards meeting your assigned duties and responsibilities? Do you only meet minimum requirements or do you aim to exceed expectations? In what ways can you improve?

3. How would your life change if you intentionally went above and beyond your required duties?

Daily Journal

Lesson 10

Be Hospitable Towards Others

What do the following scriptures teach in regard to being hospitable towards others?

Genesis 24

Deuteronomy 10:19

Hebrews 13:2

1 Peter 4:7-9

Titus 1:8

Matthew 25:40

Luke 10:38

Proverbs 18:12

Discussion Questions

1. Why is it important to be hospitable towards others?

2. In what ways did Rebecca demonstrate hospitality towards Abraham's servant?

3. Has anyone ever demonstrated hospitality towards you? If so; how did it make you feel?

4. What are some reasons that people fail to be hospitable towards others?

Self-Analysis

1. Do you currently demonstrate the level of hospitality towards others that you would want demonstrated towards you?

2. What actions can you take to become more hospitable towards others?

Daily Journal

Lesson 11

When Opportunity Knocks, Don't Delay

What do the following scriptures teach us in regard to taking advantage of opportunities?

Genesis 24

Ephesians 5:15

Ecclesiastes 3:1-11

Ecclesiastes 9:11

Discussion Questions

1. What did you learn from Rebecca on the importance of taking advantage of opportunities?

2. What are some common reasons why people refuse to take advantage of divine opportunities?

Self-Analysis

1. What opportunities have presented it self to you that you wish you could go back and take advantage of?

2. What hindered you from stepping out at that time?

3. In your opinion what was the impact of this missed opportunity on our life?

4. What steps can you take to ensure that you don't miss divine opportunities in the future?

Daily Journal

Lesson 12

Be a Woman of Your Word

What do the following scriptures teach us in regard to fulfilling our word?

1 Samuel 1:24-28

Matthew 5:33

Proverbs 12:22

Proverbs 12:14

Proverbs 6:1-3

James 4:15

Ecclesiastes 5:4-6

Numbers 30:1-4

Numbers 32:24

Discussion Questions

1. After reading the lesson on Hannah, how far do you think a person should go in regard to keeping their word?

2. Why is it important that we as daughters of God fulfill our word?

3. Has anyone ever made you a promise that they did not keep? What were your feelings towards that person?

Self-Analysis

1. Do you remember a time in your life that you made a promise or gave your word to someone and did not fulfill it? If so; how did it make you feel? How did you handle the situation?

2. After reading this lesson, what will you do in the future in regard to obligating yourself to others and keeping your word?

Daily Journal

Lesson 13

Learn to Celebrate Others' Blessings

What do the following scriptures teach us in regard to celebrating with others?

Luke 1:41-58

Proverbs 27:17

Romans 12:15

Philippians 2:1-4

1 Thessalonians 5:11-13

Discussion Questions

1. What are the benefits of celebrating the blessings of others?

2. What are some of the reasons that women refuse to celebrate with one another?

Self-Analysis

1. Has anyone ever celebrated your success or blessings? If so, how did it make you feel?

2. When was the last time you had an opportunity to celebrate someone else's' success or blessings? Did you celebrate? Why or why not?

3. What will you do differently in the future in regard to celebrating the successes and blessings of others?

Daily Journal

Lesson 14

Admit Your Mistakes

What do the following scriptures teach us in regard to admitting our wrongs?

Genesis 16

Proverbs 28:13

James 5:16

Proverbs 29:23

Jeremiah 3:13

Proverbs 11:2

Discussion Questions

1. What are some things that keep people from admitting their wrongs?

2. What are some of the consequences of not admitting our mistakes?

3. What do you think of people who find it difficult to admit their mistakes?

4. Discuss a mistake that you made in your life of which you did not readily admit to? What were the consequences?

Self-Analysis

1. If you were in a disagreement with a friend and afterwards discovered that you were wrong, how would you respond?

2. Do you readily admit your mistakes? Why or why not?

3. Are you currently dealing with mistakes or wrongs to which you have not yet acknowledged? If so, how will you respond?

Daily Journal

Lesson 15

Cultivate a Heart of Humility

What do the following scriptures teach us in regard to Humility?

Genesis 16

Proverbs 22:4

James 4:6

Luke 14:7-11

Romans 12:3

Mathew 23:12

Jeremiah 9:23-24

Proverbs 29:23

Proverbs 11:2

Proverbs 18:12

Proverbs 15:33

Proverbs 16:18

Psalm 25:9

Discussion Questions

1. What does being humble mean to you?

2. What are Gods feeling towards those who walk in pride?

3. Why did Hagar begin to look down on Sarai?

4. What are some of the things that cause people to take on a spirit of pride?

5. How did Sarai respond to Hagar's pride?

6. What are the consequences of being prideful?

7. Why should we as daughters of God walk in humility?

Self-Analysis

1. Have you ever found yourself feeling as though you were better than other people? If so, what gave you that impression?

2. Have you ever considered yourself more worthy of God's blessings than others? Why?

3. Have you ever found yourself being judgmental towards others? If so, what does this reveal concerning you?

4. Do you think that you are more deserving of God's blessings than others?

5. What actions will you take to avoid walking in pride?

Daily Journal

Lesson 16

See Beyond Your Nothings

What do the following scriptures teach us in regard to God's methods of provision?

2 Kings 4:1-7

John 2:1-10

Philippians 4:19

Matthew 14:15-20

Deuteronomy 8:18

Discussion Questions

1. What are some of the things that blind people from seeing beyond the "nothing" of their situations?

2. What does the Word of God promise us in regard to Him providing for our needs?

Self-Analysis

1. Do you remember a time when God used something you already possessed to meet your needs?

2. What special gifts, talents or abilities has God placed within you? How are you using these to meet your needs?

Daily Journal

Lesson 17

You Can't Tell Everybody Everything

What do the following scriptures teach in regard to our faith?

2 Kings 4:8-37

Hebrews 10:23

Habakkuk 2:4

Matthew 9:27-30

Mark 9:20-23

Matthew 8:5-13

Discussion Questions

1. What are some reasons that people fail to support the dreams and desires of others?

2. Why did the Shunammite woman not bury her son after his death?

3. How did the Shunammite woman's husband reply when she told him that she was going out to find the man of God? How is this response a reflection of his faith?

4. Why is it important to share your dreams and desires only with those of like faith?

Self-Analysis

1. Are there any dreams or desires that you have stopped pursuing due to the opinions of others?

2. Are there any dreams in your life in need of resurrection? If so, what are they?

3. How can you as a Christian increase the level of your faith?

4. What do you currently believe God for? Have you shared those desires with anyone else? If so, what was their response?

Daily Journal

Lesson 18

Don't Be Afraid to Cross Cultural Boundaries

What do the following scriptures teach us in regard to our dealings with others who may be different from us in some way?

John 4:1-42

Galatians 3:28

James 2:1-8

Romans 12:10

Romans 12:16

Romans 2:10-11

Romans 10:11-13

1 Corinthians 4:6-7

1 Corinthians 12:12-13

Galatians 2:6-10

Colossians 3:11

Acts 10:34-36

Matthew 13:24-30

Mark 2:16-17

Discussion Questions

1. What are some common barriers that divide people today?

2. How are personal biases towards others similar to pride?

3. What are the benefits of being open to all people?

4. What are the consequences of limiting your dealings with certain groups of people because of personal (unbiblical) biases?

5. What would the Samaritan woman have missed had she refused to communicate with Jesus due to cultural animosity? How would this have impacted her life and the lives of those in her community?

Self-Analysis

1. What type boundaries are there in your life that has led you to limit your dealings with other people?

2. How were these boundaries adapted in your life?

3. What will you do differently now that you know truth?

Daily Journal

Lesson 19

Be a Peacemaker

What do the following scriptures teach us in regard to being peacemakers?

1 Samuel 25:2-43

Matthew 5:9

Proverbs 13:10

Proverbs 10:11

Proverbs 12:20

Mark 9:50

Romans 14: 17-9

James 3:17-18

2 Corinthians 13:11

Ephesians 4:1-3

Discussion Questions

1. What does Jesus say in regard to peacemakers in Matthew 5:9?

2. What methods did Abigail use to calm David's fury? How did David respond?

3. Why was David thankful that Abigail intervened?

4. What are the consequences of anger left un-kindled?

5. How would the world be different if there were more peacemakers?

Self-Analysis

1. How do you handle disagreements with others?

2. How do you respond to people who approach you in anger?

3. Do you remember a time in your life when you witnessed discord among others? If so, what was your response? How will you respond differently in the future?

Daily Journal

Lesson 20

Determine to Leave the Past Behind

What do the following scriptures teach us in regard to leaving our past behind?

Ruth 1

2 Corinthians 5:17

Ecclesiastes 7:10

Jeremiah 29:11-13

Isaiah 43:18-19

Philippians 3:13-14

Luke 9:62

Psalm 37:23-24

2 Timothy 1:7

Discussion Questions

1. Why did Naomi urge her daughters-in-law to return to their own people after the death of their husbands? Whose interest was she concerned with?

2. What was Ruth's motive behind not returning to her past but dwelling with her mother in law? Whose interest was she concerned with?

3. What are some of the reasons that people choose to return to the past as opposed to stepping out into the unknown?

Self-Analysis

1. Are there currently any areas of your life where you recognize that it is time to leave the known and step out into the unknown? If so, what are they and what actions will you take to move forward?

Daily Journal

Lesson 21

Have Confidence in God's Words

What do the following scriptures teach us in regard to the reliability of God's Word?

Judges 4

John 1:1

Matthew 24:35

Romans 10:17

Isaiah 55:10-11

Isaiah 40:8

Psalm 147:15

Psalm 12:6-7

Psalm 119:89, 160

Job 23:12

John 2:1-10

Acts 20:32

John 2:1-10

1 Peter 1:25

Revelation 19:15

Hebrews 4:12

John 2:1-10

Jeremiah 17:7

Discussion Questions

1. Why was Deborah willing to travel to Kedesh with Barak after she received a Word of victory from God?

2. What are some of the reasons that people fail to believe Gods Word for their life?

3. Why did Barak insist on Deborah coming to Kedesh with him and his army?

4. What are the consequences of Barak's unwillingness to step out on God's Word without Deborah's company?

Self-Analysis

1. What promises has God made to you concerning your life?

2. Are you currently living your life as though you believe Gods promises to you?

3. How can you increase your confidence in the Word of God?

Daily Journal

_____
_____
_____
_____
_____
_____
_____
_____
_____
_____
_____
_____
_____
_____
_____
_____
_____
_____
_____
_____
_____
_____
_____
_____
_____
_____
_____
_____
_____
_____
_____
_____

Lesson 22

God has Equipped You
with Everything You need for Victory

What do the following scriptures teach us in regard to facing our challenges?

Deuteronomy 20:4

2 Corinthians 2:14

Philippians 4:13

Ephesians 3:20

Genesis 28:15

Psalm 18:32-34

1 Corinthians 15:57-58

Isaiah 41:10

Joshua 1:9

Deuteronomy 33:27

Psalm 60:12

Psalm 27:1

Isaiah 54:17

Jeremiah 20:11

Discussion Questions

1. What made Sisera feel safe when he entered Jael's tent?

2. What do we learn from Sisera in regard to the dangers of drawing conclusions based upon a person's outward appearances?

3. What strengths and life experiences did Jael use to kill Sisera? What gave Jael the strength to overpower a man skilled at war? How can this same source of strength be used to help you gain victory in the situations you face?

Self-Analysis

1. Describe a time in your life in which you had to face a situation that seemed overwhelming? What was the outcome?

2. As you evaluate the situation, what strengths or abilities did you use or could you have used to assist in gaining the victory?

3. After reading this lesson how will you face your challenges differently in the future?

Daily Journal

Lesson 23

Timing is Everything

What do the following scriptures teach us in regard to God's timing?

Ecclesiastes 8:5-6

Ecclesiastes 3:1-11

Habakkuk 2:3

Lamentations 3:25-26

2 Peter 3:8-9

John 2:1-10

Philippians 4:6-7

Galatians 6:9

Psalm 37:7-9

Psalm 31:15

Psalm 90:4

Discussion Questions

1. Why is it important that we wait for Gods timing in all that we pursue?

2. What are some common reasons that people prematurely step out on pursuits as opposed to waiting for Gods perfect time?

3. What are some of the consequences people face when they pursue their desires prematurely?

Self-Analysis

1. Do you recall a time in your life when your life when you stepped out prematurely? What was the outcome? What will you do differently in the future?

Daily Journal

Lesson 24

Be Persistent

What do the following scriptures teach us in regard to persistence?

Mark 7: 24-30

Galatians 6:9

Luke 11:9-10

Luke 18:1-8

Proverbs 24:16

Discussion Questions

1. How did the Greek woman respond to Jesus's initial denial of her request?

2. What are some reasons that people allow denials to discourage them from further pursuing their dreams and desires?

3. What did Jesus see in the Greek woman that caused Him to change His decision in regard to delivering her daughter?

Self-Analysis

1. How do you usually respond to denials in your life?

2. Identify three things that you desire to have or accomplish in your life?

3. What does Gods Word say in regard to these desires?

4. What action steps are required of you to achieve your desires?

5. After reading this lesson how will you respond to denials from others in regard to the fulfillment of dreams and desires promised to you by God?

Daily Journal

Lesson 25

Listen to the Wisdom of Your Elders

What do the following scriptures teach us in regard to receiving wisdom from others?

Proverbs 15:22

Proverbs 13:14

Proverbs 16:16

Proverbs 1:7-9

Proverbs 25:12

Proverbs 9:9

Proverbs 28:26

Proverbs 10:8

Ecclesiastes 1:9

Ecclesiastes 7:5

Discussion Questions

1. Why is it important to seek Godly wisdom from others?

2. What wisdom did Naomi share with Ruth to assist her in becoming the wife of Boaz? What was the result of Ruth's obedience to Godly wisdom?

3. What wisdom did Mordecai give Esther in regard to becoming Queen and saving the lives of her people from annihilation? What was the outcome of Esther's obedience to Mordecai's wisdom to her?

4. What are some reasons that people avoid asking and obeying the wisdom and directives of others?

Self-Analysis

1. How do you currently respond to the wisdom you obtain from others?

2. Do you currently have a mentor in your life? Why or why not?

3. What wisdom have you acquired from another person that has changed your life?

Daily Journal

Lesson 26

Cultivate a Heart of Gratitude

What do the following scriptures teach us in regard to having a heart of thanksgiving?

Psalm 9:1

Psalm 103:2

Psalm 100

Ephesians 3:20

Colossians 3:17

1 Thessalonians 5:18

Psalm 92:1-4

Hebrews 13:15

Colossians 2:6-7

Psalm 118

Discussion Questions

1. Why is it important to have a heart of gratitude towards God and others?

2. What are some reasons that people neglect communicating thankfulness to God?

3. What are the dangers of not being thankful to God and others?

Self-Analysis

1. In what ways do you demonstrate thanksgiving to God?

2. When your day seems not to be going the way you desire, can you usually find something to be thankful for? Why or why not?

3. During your daily communion with God do you usually spend more time making requests of God or giving Him thanks? Why?

Daily Journal

Additional Notes

_____
_____
_____
_____
_____
_____
_____
_____
_____
_____
_____
_____
_____
_____
_____
_____
_____
_____
_____
_____
_____
_____
_____
_____
_____
_____
_____
_____
_____
_____

Additional Notes

Additional Notes

Additional Notes

Additional Notes

_____
_____
_____
_____
_____
_____
_____
_____
_____
_____
_____
_____
_____
_____
_____
_____
_____
_____
_____
_____
_____
_____
_____
_____
_____
_____
_____
_____
_____
_____

Additional Notes

Additional Notes

Additional Notes

Additional Notes

Additional Notes

Additional Notes

Additional Notes

Additional Notes

Additional Notes

Additional Notes

Additional Notes

Additional Notes

Additional Notes

Additional Notes

Additional Notes

CPSIA information can be obtained
at www.ICGtesting.com
Printed in the USA
FFOW01n1341150515
13381FF